THE
FIGHTING
MAN

THE SOLDIER AT WAR
FROM THE AGE OF NAPOLEON
TO THE SECOND WORLD WAR

The FIGHTING MAN

The Soldier at War

From the Age of Napoleon to the Second World War

PAUL LEWIS ISEMONGER
&
CHRISTOPHER SCOTT

FOREWORD BY
HOWARD GILES

SUTTON PUBLISHING

First published in the United Kingdom in 1998 by
Sutton Publishing Limited · Phoenix Mill
Thrupp · Stroud · Gloucestershire · GL5 2BU

British Library Cataloguing in Publication Data

A catalogue record for this book is available from the British Library

ISBN 0 7509 1413 0

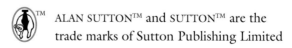 ALAN SUTTON™ and SUTTON™ are the trade marks of Sutton Publishing Limited

Typeset in 10/14 pt Galliard.
Typesetting and origination by
Sutton Publishing Limited
Printed in Great Britain by
Butler & Tanner, Frome, Somerset.

CONTENTS

FOREWORD

HOWARD GILES, HEAD OF SPECIAL EVENTS, ENGLISH HERITAGE

Since the dawn of time mankind has engaged in warfare. It has been instrumental in the forging and destruction of civilisations, mighty empires and whole cultures. Yet until the last hundred years what these great conflicts looked like was only known for sure by those fortunate – or unfortunate – participants, the soldiers, camp followers – and victims. In the pre-photographic age, any visual records of military triumphs or disasters were drawn or painted and unfortunately those depicting the conflicts of the ancient and pre-medieval world have been largely lost to us.

The later images that survive, through illuminated manuscripts, seventeenth-century woodcuts or the glorious Napoleonic canvases of Detaille, reflect no more than a partial reality. In many cases conflict is glorified, usually for the personal enhancement of a successful general or head of state. It is only when we reach the Crimea and the American Civil War that early photographs begin to show the reality of warfare, but even these take the form of individual portraits or scenes rather than a sequence of pictures representing a particular battle. Only with the introduction of combat cameramen, movie film and video has actual battle been recorded in sequence. And now the face of modern warfare in all its ugliness is instantly available to us by satellite television.

How, then, to recreate the distant past to show how a seventeenth-century battle may have looked or to recreate the circumstances by which a Victoria Cross was won during the First World War? Fortunately, this is now possible, through the creative use of the many excellent historical re-enactment societies that have sprung up all over Europe and in the United States since the embryonic beginning of the hobby in the 1960s.

Historical re-enactment has come a long way in thirty years. Once at best described as 'dressing up and having fun', the hobby has achieved major advances in both authenticity and objectives. Formerly confined to simply fighting battles, whole living history scenarios are now created. Today's re-enactment groups act as a window on the past, constantly evolving and improving as new adherents seek to portray accurately a particular era, individual or soldier. From Roman legionaries to seventeenth-century musketeers to the GIs of the Second World War, the variety of re-enactment groups is enormous. Virtually every era of European or American history is now represented, an opportunity enthusiastically grasped by agencies such as English Heritage or CADW in Britain, or individual towns and villages across Europe such as Waterloo or Leipzig, commemorating great events in their past.

The film industry has also discovered re-enactment, with fully trained, correctly clothed and equipped re-enactors playing important roles as extras in historical films and documentaries. So it was only natural that in time publishers would also utilise re-enactors to recreate either important incidents that occurred before the invention of photography or ones that could not be fully recorded by that new medium. This is exactly what Paul Lewis Isemonger and Christopher Scott's book sets out to do. In a series of striking photographs, Paul has recreated the intensity of combat aboard one of His Majesty's Ships of the Line at Trafalgar, he allows us to step into the ranks during the American Civil War and experience the Battle of Bull Run, or we can witness Sidney Bates of the Royal Norfolk Regiment winning his VC in the Second World War. All are convincingly recreated, the drama enhanced by the use of black and white film by a photographer who has cut his teeth on re-enactments all round the country, including many at English Heritage properties. The photographs are accompanied by Christopher Scott's detailed text in which the weaponry and tactics of the combatants involved are meticulously explained.

There should be more books like this and I am sure there will be. In the meantime, I commend you this first-class combination of atmospheric photography and historical fact.

Howard Giles
January 1998

ACKNOWLEDGEMENTS

CHRISTOPHER SCOTT

I would like to acknowledge all the help I have received from the Swindon Library and from my wargaming friends, as well as the information supplied from various period experts from the worlds of academia, re-enactment and both. To all who allowed me to go to them for details, whether it was among dusty tomes, by long-distance telephone or punctuated by English Heritage sponsored explosions, thank you. Particular thanks go to Donald Featherstone, who not only proffered his expertise on the Victorian soldier, but who first kindled this military interest and, with his encouragement, kept it burning over so many years. I am also grateful to Richard Ellis for his advice, military and photographic, and his discipline in not allowing me to give in to the enormity of the task and hide in the Highworth Coffee Shop. I would also acknowledge the help I had from the readers, some unknown, but especially to Richard Rutherford-Moore, whose knowledge of Napoleonic Riflemen surpasses that of anyone else I have encountered. Finally, I would like to thank my wife Pam for all her forbearance as I thought only of 'fighting men' for so long and monopolised the word processor when she needed to work on her thesis.

PAUL LEWIS ISEMONGER

An almost endless list of people helped in setting up, and participating in, the images in this book. (For further details see Useful Addresses.) To name them all would take an entire volume in itself. I hope those left out will forgive me and allow the following to take the applause on their behalf:

Richard Rutherford-Moore
Chris Collingwood
Richard Ellis
Paul Meekins
Howard Giles and the Special Events team at English Heritage
Alan Larsen and The Troop in their 17th Lancer incarnation
Jeff Carefoot, Tom Hill and all The Great War Society members
Neil Storey and the 'Royal Norfolks'
The Second World War Living History Association
Brian Perkins

'D' Company 2nd Battalion 505th Parachute Infantry Regiment, 82nd Airborne Division
5 Kompanie 916 Grenadier Regiment
No. 5 AFPS British Army Film and Photographic Unit
1st Battalion The Hampshire Regiment, 231st Brigade, 50th (Northumbrian) Division
Mark Patman and Paul Woodadge for organising the English Heritage Operation Fortitude-South event at Dover Castle

Kriegsmarine Association – UK

Princess Irenes Group – Netherlands

The Garrison Living History Group

Sword Battery, Royal Artillery Display Team

Jef Savage, John Rayner, Roy Daines and the Southern Skirmish Association

Clive Green and The 4th Michigan Volunteer Cavalry

Chris Jones and the Historical Maritime Society – sailors, officers, civilians and Royal Marines

Blaise Viner and The Trincomalee Trust

Hartlepool Historic Quay, a Flagship Scheme of the Teesside Development Corporation

Chris Durkin

Mike Freeman

Ted Peacock

Glen Robinson

Mike Grove

Keith Phillips

Les Handscombe

Norman Stringer

Malcolm McDonald

Tim Rose and the Diehard Company

Paul Weaver

Annie

Steve and Liz at HDP

John Wilson for help with software problems

Midas for computer problem solving

Sharon Lockyer for computer operations and endless scanning

Jason Lockyer, cabinet maker, for producing a faithful working reproduction of a sliding-box camera for the book launch

Joan and Marilyn

This book would not have been possible without the stunning realism and the attention to detail of the world of re-enactment. The preparation of the images for this book has allowed me to stand on board a Napoleonic period British Naval Frigate as she is prepared for sea; to listen to a 'Docksy' as she propositions a newly-paid seaman; to stand in front of a 17th Lancer as he charges his horse towards me, lance lowered. I have been recruited by The 4th Michigan Volunteer Cavalry to fight for the North (my friends in the South will never forgive me); listened to the banter of Tommies in the dark muddy trenches, sharing their half-cold tea, and then witnessed the disciplined bravery of a dawn raid across 'No Man's Land', cutting my hand on barbed wire as I followed them into the dawn. I have watched the winning of a Victoria Cross as the Allies make their steady and bloody progress after D-Day in 1944. What has struck me time and time again throughout these experiences is how 'right' the faces often seem to be. If I believed in reincarnation I might be tempted to think that these re-enacted scenes come from the experience of the real thing in a previous life. The reality is that these men and women have a genuine feel for their period and a deep respect for the Fighting Man. It shows.

INTRODUCTION

Human beings have an aggressive aspect to their nature; not the most pleasant of attributes but surely one of the most successful in ensuring the survival of the species, even if it has meant the extermination of large proportions of it. When threatened, the human animal experiences a flow of various hormones that usually prepares the body for extreme action, be it running away or fighting. When a man is angered, energy-carrying blood drains from the superfluous regions, such as the face, as it is pumped to the muscles in the limbs indicating that the body is getting ready to fight in basic self-preservation. In addition to defending themselves, men and women have fought over food, possessions, territory and the betterment of their social groups. As communities evolved, the sense of belonging to a particular group transmogrified the nature and style of their fighting, hence different cultures produced different ways of combating each other in groups. To those who have grown up with television news footage and films of Vietnam, The Falklands, Afghanistan, the Gulf and Bosnia, the tribal wars filmed on Papua New Guinea in the 1920s may not look like war, more like ritualistic skirmishes, with unified chanting, dancing and provocative gesturing interspersed with rare flashes of violent action, but to the participants it was very real warfare.

As community-living developed, so traditionally the young people, the most fit and most active of the tribe, did its fighting and, because the risk of life and limb was great, so too were the rewards they gained. The fighters were accorded deference, adopted distinguishing dress and elaborate artistic motifs; they had menial tasks performed for them and, when not in arms, were permitted a life of relative ease. As 'might' became the deciding factor in the social pecking order, a warrior class emerged. They chose how, where and when wars were to be waged, and evolved codes of behaviour, methods of training and, much later, manuals to govern and teach the art of operating their violence-based lifestyle. They held power; their families accrued esteem, land and wealth over others and this was often made public through artistic display, such as the European obsession with heraldry. Even in each family group, because of his general physical prowess, the role of the fighter-hunter devolved upon the male of the species – but probably not so firmly as Victorian historians and illustrators would have us believe. However, the fighting man with his art of war has become a traditional component in most societies around the globe and across the pages of time, but his story has been intertwined with two others; technology and teamwork.

The human animal is very limited in personal combat capabilities. We can inflict damage with our hands and feet by punching and kicking, we can use our foreheads or our knees but, unlike many other animals, we do not have built-in weapons such as claws, and our teeth are of little use. Human

intellect has enabled us to use and develop weapons and armour to enhance our capability to inflict and limit damage. The types and styles of these artefacts are culturally derived, and warriors are dependent upon the thinkers, inventors, engineers and craftspeople whom they traditionally regard as social inferiors. Warrior effectiveness has rarely been measured devoid of arms and armour, and history should perhaps be interpreted as the progress of famous technological advances rather than the martial deeds of people. The development of the smelting process to produce iron swords, which cut through and buckled bronze, could be said to have had a greater influence on warfare than the individuals who wielded them. As technology progressed it made dramatic changes to the way people fought and how armies were constituted, looked and behaved. The warriors might have evolved the art of war but technology made it a science.

As conflicts grew, so did the necessity for wider participation. Rousing the desire to fight in the non-warrior classes became essential. Nationalism and religion have helped many politicians unite tribes, peoples and cultures to swell the ranks of armies. Greater numbers increase the chance of winning, but do not guarantee success. People need to work together towards a common aim if they are to achieve it. The mastering of the warrior élite by social and physical inferiors acting in unison is another great theme of history. The ways in which people came together to fight, how they cooperated with each other, and how their weapons were deployed in group actions, proved that disciplined and well-drilled bodies of men could triumph over the exceptional bravery and martial prowess of the few. When strongly motivated group action was combined with scientific advances in armaments and communications, the result was the concept of the nation in arms. As huge conscript armies, deployed in massed formations, hit each other with all the technologically superior force their homeland factories and farms can manufacture or produce, and their transport systems deliver, we move into the industry of war, which is, in turn, but a short step to regarding war as a continuation of politics, devoting whole economies, industries and people to the war effort. Civilians become logistical targets and the fighting man simply a component part of total war. Battles have always been won by the makers, the growers and the carriers as well as by the men and their warrior heroes in the fighting line.

The story of armies through the ages has three main elements – the people who comprised them, the technological advances they epitomised and the teamwork tactics they adopted – and it describes how these three factors varied in importance, the complicated balancing act they performed and the effect this had on human unhumanity. While not disregarding the other components, this book seeks to concentrate on the age of the great technology race, as nations sought to outdo one another in the modernisation of weaponry, and to harness national budgets and workforces in the mass production of weapons, with every new innovation incorporated as it was discovered.

Technological innovation is a tale of both surprising as well as logical solutions to problems, and revolves around the competitive desire to gain an advantage in the grisly business of killing. Although complex and complicated in its detail, the process falls into a simple pattern that makes the understanding of military history far easier than many people think. There have been two major technological changes in the deadly industry that is warfare. The first was the introduction of gunpowder weapons, which dramatically changed the nature of warfare, wresting it from the military warrior élite and giving supremacy to common soldiers. The second change was the gearing of modern industrial processes to weaponry, which dramatically increased the range and speed at which men could kill. Both changes were revolutionary in their effects upon war and the men who fought them.

The content of this publication is limited by the range of periods that British battle and living history re-enactors have chosen to portray. There were conflicts all over the world and although they are missing from these pages, it is not by way of intention to belittle their contribution or impact or to suggest that they are undeserving of mention. Beginning with the supremacy of the smoothbore Brown Bess on the fields of Waterloo, this work looks at the way men coped with weapons that changed dramatically, enabling them to fight hundreds of yards apart. It examines the way in which scientific research and development programmes made the killing faster and even more distant, and enabled men from the industrial towns of European powers to create empires across the globe in epic, though uneven, struggles against native populations in Asia, Africa and Australasia. The book also considers how war became industrialised, how soldiers became instruments of foreign policy, and how battlefields grew in size, scale and diversity of climate until the world powers finally turned on each other in the

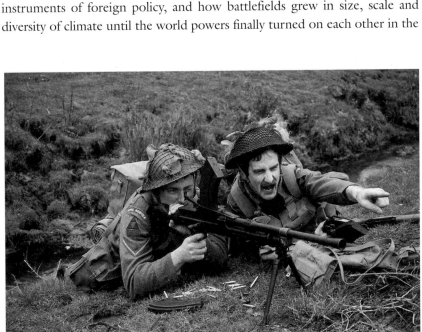

blood-soaked mud of Flanders – the Great War. It ends with the mechanisation of weapons, soldiers and nations in the conflict known as the Second World War.

However, above all this is a story about people, about soldiers who go about the business of killing each other and whose arsenals give them greater ability to fight further and further apart. As the fighting becomes more detached, we can focus more upon the common soldier through the ages. During the sixties, it was fashionable to speak about the universality of the common soldier but, as the weapons changed, the nature of war changed and the men changed too. The warrior social élite was replaced by despised professionals who in turn handed over to whole nations in arms.

THE NAPOLEONIC WARS

THE NAPOLEONIC WARS

The term 'Napoleonic' Wars is a somewhat popular misnomer, as it was not until the end of his military career that foreign populations thought of 'The Emperor' as the prime mover in the conflicts that dominated the early nineteenth century. Napoleon inherited a European struggle that began with the French Revolution in 1789. The American War of Independence had fostered ideas of democracy and social justice, and soldiers returning from France's involvement in that conflict brought those ideas home, along with the notion that even the most powerful can be defeated by the united will of a people. The ensuing revolution was a political watershed as the success of a republican insurrection against its monarch sent shock waves throughout the 'civilised world'. Although the urban mob was the force factor, it was manipulated by the educated middle class, who wanted a share in the government and the power. England had gone through this crisis in the 1640s and its king had gone to the block as a result. France followed in the 1790s and caused the other monarchs of Europe to look warily over their shoulders at their own rich, articulate and frustrated intellectuals. Foreign wars are excellent political expedients for uniting a troubled country, especially those that can apparently be easily won. So the various European monarchies entered a Coalition against Revolutionary France with the intention of returning her to her 'imprisoned king' and showing the rest of the world that established and powerful regimes could not, and should not, be overthrown by lesser orders without restoration and retribution.

'The Emperor'

The old royal armies of Austria, Prussia, Russia, along with those of the various confederations of kings, princes, dukes, electors and margraves, etc., throughout northern and central Europe, banded together in a series of political treaties to attack France and her citizen army, ruled by a citizen government. The French replied with an almost crusader-like zeal to spread *Liberté* and *Egalité* abroad, and if their opposing soldiers would not welcome *Fraternité* with open arms, then they could embrace their bayonets! However, their first campaign went badly. Rochambeau, victor in America, could do little to prevent them being repulsed from the proposed invasion of the Austrian Netherlands (Belgium). In defence of their homeland they stood at Valmy (1792) and the old royal army gunners caused the allies to withdraw. Elsewhere they had better fortune, especially in the taking of Nice and Savoy while Dumouriez took Brussels, although Custine's invasion of Germany reached Frankfurt and then got pinned back behind the Rhine.

The execution of Louis XVI in 1793 and the threat to European trade brought Britain and Holland, and their wealth, into the war, along with Spain, Portugal, Naples and Tuscany. The First Coalition was in place and ready to fight the new left-wing ideology. Allied successes meant an end to political and career hopes for the unlucky French generals and Dumouriez followed Lafayette into the allied camp, while Custine went to the guillotine. France succumbed to 'the Terror' and an anti-revolutionary rebellion broke out in the Vendée. Romantics tell that the French 'revolutionary spirit' won several battles for them in 1794 but more likely it was the impact of Carnot's reforms and their desperate fight for self-preservation against enemies all around them. The war in the Netherlands continued during 1795, with Pichegru capturing the ice-bound Dutch fleet, and Holland broke free of its old rulers to form the French-inspired Batavian Republic. Meanwhile, Prussia's efforts ground to a halt, the *émigrés* and British were defeated at Quiberon, Spain and the German States made peace, Hoche brutally crushed the Vendéan rebels and the Austrians were fought to a standstill in Italy by Messena. However, even these successes could not extinguish insurrection, and a royalist rising in Paris gave a military and political opportunity to a young Corsican artillery general called Bonaparte. France needed to cross frontiers – to stop its defensive mentality, to spread the revolutionary gospel and, above all, to feed and equip its growing army from the farms and coffers of its enemies.

Bonaparte was sent to Italy in 1796 where he fought both the Piedmontese and the Austrian armies in a seventeen-day lightning campaign of strike and manoeuvre, which resulted in the conquest of Lombardy and ensured the

future cooperation of Nice, Savoy, Piedmonte and the northern Italian States. On one occasion Napoleon led a bayonet charge across the bridge at Lodi and gave birth to the legend of glory, bravery and the sharing of a soldier's dangers that he was to nurture and promote for the rest of his career. By the end of the year, with battles at Lonato, Castiglione and Arcola, he had broken Austrian supremacy in Italy which he further exploited in '97, driving the Austrians back into their homeland and out of the war. Without referring to the government, Napoleon dictated the surrender terms himself, annexing the Austrian Netherlands and creating the pro-French Cisalpine Republic in north Italy. He was moving skilfully into the political field and fast becoming a 'major player'.

Spain had defected to the French camp in '96 but the British navy sunk her fleet off Cape St Vincent in February '97 and also sunk the Dutch fleet at Camperdown in October. France suffered a *coup d'état* from a government backed by Bonaparte and the army. In return, he got permission to invade Egypt in order to threaten British India and to send a force to Ireland. Both took place in '98 and both failed due to an inability to reinforce and because of local resistance, although Napoleon made gains and won several victories. However, by the end of '98 Russia, Austria, Britain, Portugal, Naples, the Vatican and the Ottoman Empire had created the Second Coalition, which almost cleared Italy of the 'French infestation', but poor liaison dogged operations in the low countries and Switzerland became the scene of several bloody slogging matches. Russia withdrew in disgust in '99 and Bonaparte staged a lightning coup by returning from Egypt and politically manoeuvring to establish the Consulate, backed by the army with himself as 'First Consul' or virtual dictator.

French power frightened the British government, and, fearing for Britain's trade in India, it ordered a young general Wellesley to crush French influence in Mysore while it continued to pour money into the European war. Bonaparte quickly took control of all France's war efforts and, in 1800, he flung himself energetically into the campaign in Italy, which he won by rapid manoeuvre and his soldiers' stubborn determination to fight against the odds. He switched attention and directed the fight against Austria in Germany. By the end of the year, Austria sued for peace and the Second Coalition collapsed. Treaties, international politics, boycotts and trade agreements followed, which isolated Britain. The Royal Navy responded by sinking the Danish fleet in Copenhagen and severely damaging the Franco-Spanish fleet at Algeciras. They also ferried Abercromby to the successful relief of Egypt and put an end to any French 'Eastern aspirations'. In 1802 peace was declared formally and Bonaparte made himself Consul for life, which he 'upgraded' to Emperor by crowning himself in 1804. However, the allied powers were not disposed to allow the seed of democracy to flower even though it cloaked itself in all the trappings of a classical monarchy, and the French-established satellite states were tempting pickings. The Third Coalition was formed.

Napoleon responded with his usual administrative alacrity and was soon at war with most of Europe. He managed to drag in as willing, and sometimes reluctant, allies all his satellite states and those who feared his 'attention' if they did not join him. From 1805 to 1814 he gradually won and then lost Europe. His troops marched from Lisbon to Moscow, from Riga to Naples, and created kingdoms and duchies in their wake. His brothers rode in triumph behind him and became kings of countries in his Empire. Many of the tiny German states along the Rhine were confederated and whole regions, such as Poland, were liberated from their foreign masters. Each of these domains produced soldiers and soon the 'French army' was more foreign than French. This was very satisfactory in victory as it paid the butcher's bill, but in adversity it caused problems, as they had little to gain from preserving French interests. Stunning victories such as Austerlitz, Jena-Auerstadt and Friedland broke the Third Coalition and brought Prussia and Russia to the peace table while Medellin and Ocana secured Spain.

It was Britain's mastery of the seas, confirmed by Trafalgar, and its economic power that kept resistance alive, and British diplomats who forged yet another Coalition to fight, although Austria declined. Napoleon spread his army so thinly that even with vast recruitment drives and pressing men into service it could not 'police' the territory it took. This was made even more difficult by campaigns further afield as the 'revolution' was carried into Portugal and Russia. The Peninsular became 'the Spanish ulcer', which sapped the Empire of men for very little financial or propaganda returns. The invasion of Russia was even worse. Both theatres soaked up manpower as the men struggled and fought through broiling heat or freezing cold and spilled their blood in uninspiring battering matches such as Fuentes d'Onoro and Borodino, or were defeated in tactical reverses such as Salamanca and Marojaroslavitz. The French Empire was assaulted on all sides and even a brief, uneasy truce in mid-1813 was a ruse to allow the allies to regroup and bring Austria again into the war. The dreadful bloodbaths of Dresden and Leipzig and the disaster of Vittoria drove the French back until, in 1814, they were defending France itself. Again Napoleon administered a strategically brilliant campaign, but not even the tactical victories of Champaubert, Montmirail and Vauchamps could stop the numerically superior allied advance. Neither could Soult defend the Pyrenees against Wellington. The Empire was crushed, the dream broken and the French fought in vain to keep the allies out of Paris and Toulouse. Napoleon's subsequent abdication and exile to Elba could not kill the 'glorious vision', and his return and Hundred Days' campaign caught Europe napping. The rout and destruction of the remains of the French Imperial forces at Waterloo sealed the fate of the Emperor but not the dream. France reverted to a monarchy, but it was not to last.

THE MEN

The early French Republic's Army was quite unprepared for the war its government declared in 1791. It had lost most of its officers through deliberate deposition and emigration. Many old soldiers too had drifted away

La Haie Sainte, Waterloo, scene of a fierce struggle during the battle of Waterloo. Major Baring and his King's German Guard staunchly defended the farmhouse until they ran out of ammunition. Of the 360 men, only 39 escaped with Baring after a bloody hand-to-hand fight

from the colours because of loyalty to the old royal cause and lack of pay and provender. To back up these much depleted old regiments, vast numbers of volunteers and conscripts were drafted into new battalions; but they were almost useless products of the *levée en masse*, whose indiscriminate and often corrupt practices lumped the most unsuitable men together, issued them with redundant and frequently broken weapons, and called them soldiers. The early campaigns were fought by a puzzling collection of older regulars, who could be relied upon to do what was required, and a jumble of formations composed of the untrained or the semi-trained displaying widely varying degrees of enthusiasm. Their attempt on Belgium was a military disaster and even Lafayette, the popular hero who succeeded their old General Rochambeau, could not politically control them. By 1795 Carnot's 'Amalgame' was mixing regulars and recruits together which meant a better distribution of experience and expertise and a levelling of battalion reliability.

Gradually, this mixture of recruits and regulars in the French army equalled that in the armies of their enemies, and, indeed, their succession of campaigns, switched from one theatre of war to another, and their almost rapid accumulation of notable victories transformed many of them into veterans. By the time Napoleon's political ambitions began to encompass the notion of a united Europe, albeit under total French suzerainty, he had many battle-hardened veteran battalions and the first nation in arms.

How battalions and regiment were organised varied from country to country; it was often the established practice that held sway, or a new commander's initiative. Napoleon ordered several changes, including the flexible demi-brigade system, until he perfected his combined arms Corps. The following are ideal set-ups with nominal, paper-strength figures:

Infantry:
British Rifle Company Organisation:

25 men + 2 NCOs = I squad. 2 squads + 2 Offs & bugler = I platoon.
2 platoons + Co. HQ of 3 Offs & 2 NCOs = I Company.

British: 60 men = I coy. 10 coys = I batt/regt. 3 regts = I brig. 3 brigs + I battery art = I div.
4/7 divs = cav arm = Army. (Sometimes each division also had a rifle company attached.)

French: 90 men = I coy. 6 coys = I batt. 3/6 batts = I regt. 2 regts = I brig. 2 brigs = I div.
3 divs + 4 regts cav + I battery art = I Corps. 2/7 Corps = cav & art reserves = Army.

Cavalry:
British: 60 men = I trp. 2 trps = I sqd. 4 sqds = I regt. 2/4 regts + I HA batt = I brig.
2/3 brigs = div.

French: 30 men = I trp. 2 trps = I coy. 2 coys = I sqd. 4/6/8 sqds = I regt. 4/7 regts + I HA batt = I brig.
2 brigs = I div.

Artillery:
British: 12 men = I gun. 2 guns = I div. 3 divs = I battery or brig.
French: 14 men = I gun. 2 guns = I section. 4 sections = I battery or coy.

Although some armies had good professional units with 'mercenary gentlemen' officers, they were too small to match or deal with 'nations in arms'. So massive recruitment from the ordinary population was required, and so too were the means of turning these into soldiers. Most European armies had strict codes of discipline designed to keep the men in line and in awe. Those conscripted by lottery or from the prisons had no choice but to accept their fate or die as deserters, and peasant soldiers were supposedly used to being treated like cattle, goaded and prodded into action, and taught the basic drills for firing the simple and often inefficient weapons they were issued. French soldiers were initially something different. Citizen volunteers had to be treated differently and led by example by brave men, not driven like sheep by fools. Most French soldiers knew their company officers; they were often from the same village, often recruited by them, and accustomed to sharing lodgings and provisions together. From diaries we can deduce that there was a mutual respect and frequently a genuine filial affection between the men and the officers. Napoleon was not averse to tweaking the cheeks of his beloved Guard Grenadiers. In the British Army it was very different. Social class separated the gentlemen from the scum, but it was a barrier wanted by both sides and consequently seldom crossed. The officers made decisions and gave the orders but it was the NCOs who implemented them. Sergeants and corporals ran the companies and the sergeant major ran the battalion; and they ran them by demanding, and getting, blind obedience to regulations. The British Napoleonic soldier's life was harsh, and possibly more so than that of his counterparts in the Austrian or Prussian armies. The rule of the NCOs was totally supported by the officers. The Duke of York's early reforms had ensured a core of proficient officers who saw to it that all ran smoothly. However, there also existed an attitude that a gentleman had 'better things' to do than be a professional soldier – hunting, balls, gaming, drinking and 'doing the season' were consuming passions that generally eclipsed some senior officers' part-time, uniform-wearing military duties.

In the French Army, discipline was purportedly maintained through respect, loyalty and desire to serve the Emperor and France. However, in most other European armies discipline was kept by punishment and that usually meant the lash. Floggings were carried out with the infamous cat-o'-nine-tails, the knotted cords of which could reduce a man's back to shredded, bleeding meat in minutes. Sentences of a couple of hundred lashes were not uncommon. Being tied to a wagon wheel for hours – a painful experience similar to a crucifixion position – was the lesser of the evils inflicted. The rationale used to defend these practices was that battle generates extreme fear and, if a man is to survive, he must obey the orders given him – obedience is the narrow thread that leads out of the dark labyrinth of panic into the light of survival. It may be true. The fact remains that the men were treated brutally and they responded to their foes in kind, with a particular savagery that became legendary.

Away from the battle, soldiers' lives across Europe were squalid in barracks and miserable in the field, made bearable by camaraderie. Crowded into large but stuffy rooms, they slept in rows of narrow beds with little

45ème de ligne, 1808–09

21ème de ligne, 1812–15

3rd Battalion 1ˢᵗ Foot Guards

space between them and only a chest beneath them for personal effects. In times of keen recruitment they sometimes had two in a bed, 'top'n'tailin', and lived a very public existence indeed. Privacy was unheard of, even the married men allowed by the British to keep their wives in barracks only had a curtain stretched across the corner of a room. Behind this woollen wall they carried out their married lives as best they could, which included having babies and raising the surviving children. The NCOs kept drumming drill and regulations into the soldiers until they could perform every move and exercise like an automaton. If stationed unexpectedly near his own village, a French soldier could live at home, as long as he was always present when required and took several of his companions with him, for whom, of course, the company no longer had to pay. Route marches and parades broke the monotomy, but wartime provided intervals of excitement and adventure.

Many books have been devoted to Napoleonic uniforms. Suffice it to say that no matter the army, style and parade ground fashion influenced what the men were supposed to wear, but that all went to pieces on campaign, sometimes literally. British scarlet faded to brick-red in the Spanish sun, Russian green could appear almost black when issued and apple-green a year later, and the indigo in French coats was known to run, staining the men's shirts and white breeches. Wellington reputedly stated he did not care what his men looked like as long as they fought well. Several Austrian generals, on

Social class separated the gentlemen from the 'scum'; it was a barrier wanted by both sides and consequently seldom crossed

At Quatre Bras in 1815, the 42nd Royal Highland Regiment were overrun by cavalry and lost 314 men and 24 officers. Two days later, unbowed, they faced the French at Waterloo

Captain of the 42nd Royal Highland Regiment

the other hand, insisted the men kept their white coats clean, while a popular anecdote tells of a Prussian officer ordering his men to clean their buttons during an action. Some nations and individual officers insisted on the high leather stock being worn in the field; it rubbed the neck and cut into the throat, leaving a rash and open sores. To test durability, a British brigadier ordered his three regiments to dress in linen breeches, wool trousers and canvas overalls respectively. Within three months campaigning the breeches were in rags, the trousers were out at the knees and the overalls reasonably intact. The men in the canvas suffered terribly from the heat and from chaffing but it was canvas replacements that were sought for the other units. More often than not, cheap brown Spanish wool served as trouser materials for all the Allied armies in the Peninsular.

Loyalty to a nation or a cause was expected and taken for granted and although this was sometimes misguided, loyalty to a unit was an almost spiritual affiliation. It was embodied in the Regimental Colours or the Eagle. The infantry regiments of most nations carried two Colours – one for the monarch and one for the unit. They were the soul of the regiment, its past and its honour. Their position in battle was important. They had to be an inspiration; they had to lead; and they had to be where the danger was greatest. Their importance could not be dismissed; it was the intricate woven silk itself that could inspire men to deeds of great heroism and self-sacrifice. To the French, the Colour they carried was very important but their pride and love was centred upon the Eagle, presented to them by the

Emperor himself. The Eagle was a gold-leafed representational figurine that grasped a thunderbolt in its claws and stood upon a plinth onto which was rivetted the regiment's number. Carrying these hallowed artefacts were young Ensigns sworn to die in their defence, a promise they frequently kept. The cavalry had their guidons and their kettledrums as objects of veneration and inspiration while the artillery had their guns.

Another inspiration for the men was music provided by the regimental musicians. Every unit had drummers, including the cavalry. They were a practical necessity for relaying orders and keeping the beat on the march, but the French and several other European nations fielded complete military bands who played stirring compositions on the march and even in action. Line infantry had fifes to supply the melody to the drums, while the Highland and some Irish regiments had their pipes. Many tales are told of brave pipers, such as George Clarke of the 71st at Vimeiro, leading their units into action and continuing to play even when desperately wounded, lest the men should falter. Armed only with chanters, they wove enchantment, and instilled fear into their foes.

A great deal too has been written about British riflemen and, although splendid troops, they were neither superhuman nor sharpshooters. Where the riflemen did come into their own, especially the green-cockaded marksmen, was in picking off French officers as they advanced with the column. The relationship enjoyed by the French officers with their men made them preferred targets. The conscript who sees the man who recruited him, shared his mess, tent, and life with him, lying dead in the Spanish dust is more demoralised than his British counterpart who, used to the rigid class division, has little affection for his officers. The French soon learnt to retaliate by shooting the British NCOs but their task was more difficult because the NCOs did not stand out so well, either by position in the line or by their uniform.

On campaign the men sometimes used tents, laid out in neat rows with streets and a 'canteen', but more usually they slept in 'quarters'. These were buildings commandeered by the provost marshal and allocated on a regimental basis – it might be a street of houses, a church, a barn, a run of huts or part of a castle, depending on what was available. The officers always took the best accommodation and established their mess. They usually fared well, dining on recently shot game and the pick of the farms and orchards; mess-servants travelled with canteens of cutlery, cases of fine wines and even some regimental silver. Wellington's various Major-Generals kept Division messes each of which had a reputation among the young officers in a strict sliding scale of excellence and status. The men got what the commissariat managed to procure for them. Their staple diet was baked hard tack, a flour and water mix attractively misnamed 'biscuit', and dried meat, and both needed soaking before eating. Stewed with vegetables grubbed from a nearby garden and washed down with copious draughts of cheap wine liberated from their 'hosts', these basic elements made a decent

The French Eagle presented to the Regiment by the Emperor

On campaign it was not unusual for men to live in tents, laid out in neat rows with streets and a 'canteen'

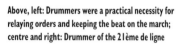

Above, left: Drummers were a practical necessity for relaying orders and keeping the beat on the march; centre and right: Drummer of the 21ème de ligne

Armed only with chanters, the pipers led their units into action. They wove enchantment while instilling fear into their foes

Above, left: The 95th Rifles were a skirmishing force – able to work independently from the main body of troops, using cover wherever possible; right: Back pack of the 95th Rifles

Left: The 95th wore a 'Rifle Green' uniform with black facings, a basic camouflage and a stovepipe hat; right: The 95th had three battalions; they usually served as one unit

meal. A frequent dish was 'stirabout' – everything in the men's haversacks thrown in a pot with porridge oats and bubbled away and stirred until pronounced 'done'. British daily rations were 1½ lb of flour or bread or 1 lb of biscuits, 1 lb of beef or ½ lb of pork including bone, ¼ pint peas or beans, 1 oz of rice and 1 oz of cheese or butter. The rations were issued when and if available; always available were liberal quantities of gin. Imported from Holland and sold at a penny a pint it was not beyond even a British government to purchase. Swigged out of tin mugs just before a battle, this 'genever' gave the men 'Dutch courage'. The men often had gin or Spanish brandy in their canteens rather than stale water. These wooden flasks hardly kept liquids cool and infection free, so spirit alcohol was a much healthier option, even if it did promote dehydration.

Each encampment had its share of campfollowers. Traders in everything, swindlers and thieves followed the armies only to discover the soldiers could out-con, out-cheat and out-swindle the lot of them, and then out-fight them if they protested. Prostitutes were numerous and many became respectable army 'wives', acquiring a new husband each time the old one died. A few officers even took their ladies with them but more often they were accompanied by local girls eager to secure a match and an escape from the humdrum poverty of their own existence. Harry Smith, a young Rifles officer, rescued a beautiful Spanish girl from the chaos of Badajoz. She went with him everywhere, married him and, in time, when he became a knight, became Lady Smith, after whom a famous South African town was named, and whose name is a battle honour for the British Army.

Officers may have had the ability to purchase their commissions and subsequent promotions through the ranks but not all were from the same mould as Harry Smith. Too often, temperamentally ill-suited and inept men rose to positions of command significance – if Erskine was bad, then Slade

Below, left: Prostitutes were numerous and many became respectable 'wives', acquiring a new husband on the death of the previous one; centre and right: Some officers took their ladies on campaign

was mad. Men could rise from the ranks but it was rare and 'command does not suit ignorant and course-minded men'. Wellington agreed with Rifleman Harris about promotions from the ranks and did not approve. He knew his soldiers came from the dregs of society, but when he called them 'the scum of the earth' he added the often forgotten phrase, 'it is really wonderful that we should have made them, such fine fellows they are'.

THEIR WEAPONS

Muskets: Most infantrymen carried a smooth-bore, flintlock musket during the Napoleonic Wars. They were all single-shot muzzle-loaders and fired by soldiers using paper cartridges. These were made from pieces of parallelogram-shaped greased paper wrapped around a stick, and twisted or glued into a tube. A measured charge was poured into the tube and a lead ball put on top of it. The end was then folded over and glued or sometimes stitched down. Each man carried about sixty of these cartridges in his cartridge pouch, the wide strap of which was slung over his shoulder, while the pouch rested on his right rear hip. When ordered to load, he half-cocked his lock to get the hammer out of the way and then lifted the leather flap of the pouch and extracted one cartridge. He conveyed it to his mouth and would bite the 'blunt end' to tear open the paper tube, often getting the acrid, salty powder into his mouth. He then used a pinch of the powder to fill his pan and snapped the frizzen-cum-pan-cover over it to keep this primer in place. Reversing his musket, he poured the remainder of the powder down the barrel and crumpled the empty cartridge with the bullet at the end into the muzzle. Taking out his steel ramrod he then rammed home, holding the rod between finger and thumb, giving two sharp taps when he was sure it was at the bottom, to compress the charge in the chamber. Experienced soldiers usually tapped their ramrods with the flat of their hands after they had put them back in their pipes to hear the reassuring 'clack' which told them they had not left it down the barrel. They would then often lick their index finger and run it along the edge of their flint to clean it ready for a good strike. With biting off and flint cleaning, their mouths must have been black after a few rounds and full of the foul-tasting spent powder. The musket was thus loaded and only needed the hammer to be pulled back onto full cock before it could be fired.

Squeezing the trigger released the cocked and trigger-sprung hammer, which held a flint in its jaws. The action of the hammer caused this flint to fly forward and scrape down the tempered frizzen, and, at the same time, open the pan-cover. The scraping flint sent a shower of sparks into the gunpowder-primed musket pan, and the resulting flash communicated through the touch-hole into the chamber of the weapon where it ignited the main charge. The expanded gases forced the ball out of the muzzle at over 500 mph, and delivered a hearty thump to the shoulder with the

Wellington did not approve of promotions from the ranks and such moves were rare, most officers coming from the 'landed gentry'

GUNPOWDER

Gunpowder is a mixture of Saltpetre, charcoal and sulphur, most usually in the proportion of 75:15:10. Saltpetre, when burned, provides the oxygen; charcoal and sulphur, the fuel. Sulphur accelerates the process, burning as it does, at a low temperature. On a flat surface without construction, gunpowder will burn readily and very fast, creating a flare with a lot of smoke. If the gunpowder is placed in a confined space and compressed, this rapid burning becomes an explosion of considerable force, sending a musket ball out of the barrel at over 500 mph.

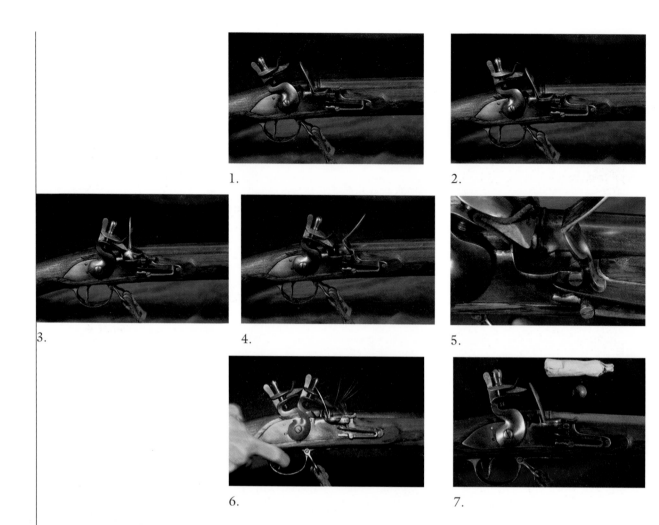

1.

2.

3.

4.

5.

6.

7.

1. 'Cocked' ready for firing
2. The trigger is pulled and the cock descends to the frizzen or strikng plate, propelled by a strong spring
3. The flint strikes the frizzen, forcing it forwards and revealing the powder in the pan
4. The sparks caused by the friction between flint and frizzen ignite the priming powder
5. The touch hole can be seen at the back of the pan on the side of the barrel. This narrow tube carries the fire into the main charge inside the barrel
6. The complete sequence showing the sparks heading for the open pan
7. Above: Paper cartridge; centre: the lead ball; below: the Brown Bess flintlock mechanism

recoil. Diaries report that after repeated firing in action, men had bruised and tender shoulders for days.

At this point in the technology race, smooth-bore muskets had not developed very far from the firearms of the previous 300 years; they were still a metal tube secured to a piece of wood using gunpowder to explode and propel a lead ball. They still had the same range as those used in the mid-seventeenth century, that is, about 300 yd, and the same accuracy factors. The ignition system of the flintlock in the early 1700s was a great improvement, but the musket of the Napoleonic era, even the famous Brown Bess, was still a barn-door weapon that relied upon massed fire rather than individual accuracy. The last thing a soldier wants in action is a jammed ball, which would render the weapon useless, so they were cast slightly smaller than the calibre of the barrel. However, this had the effect of rattling the ball up the tube, and as it left the muzzle it would fly out at the angle of the last deflection of its bouncing journey. The Brown Bess was better bored than many of its European counterparts, and some were so well bored as to warrant their being fitted with sights for some light infantry units. However, most of these smooth-bores suffered from poor accuracy.

1.

2.

1. The frizzen is pushed forward
2. A cartridge is taken from the cartridge pouch
3. The end of the cartridge is bitten off
4. The powder is poured into the barrel . . .
5. . . . followed by the lead ball and cartridge paper, which acts as wadding
6. The ramrod is withdrawn from beneath the barrel
7. The charge is rammed
8. The ramrod is replaced and 'tapped' to ensure that it has not been left in the barrel. During the heat of battle it was not unknown for the ramrod to be left in the barrel and fired at the enemy. This rendered the weapon useless unless another could be acquired

3.

4.

5.

6.

7.

8.

Accuracy, even for 'aimed' shots was erratic. There were usually no sights, although men could 'second guess' off the bayonet locking lug to achieve a quasi 'point of aim'. At 100 to 150 yd, muskets tended to fire 1 ft higher than this 'point of aim'. At 200 yd, aim and hit points were roughly the same but at 250 yd, the ball would strike 3 to 6 ft lower than where it was aimed. So, firing at over 200 yd meant 'aiming' over the enemy's head, which was a chancy business. The 'trick' was to wait to 200 yd for the first round and aim at a man's chest (crossbelts made a good target indicator); at 150 yd aim at the groin; at 100 yd the knees; and at less than 100 yd but more than 50 yd, the feet. Less than 50 yd and the trajectory was fairly straight, but it was best to aim low to allow for bouncing the ball through an enemy's shins.

The main weapon of the French soldier was the Modele 1777 smooth-bore musket, mostly manufactured at Charleville. It went through several modifications but was always easily distinguishable by the iron fittings and the brass bands that held the barrel to the stock, especially the distinctive, wide and divided fore-end band. It was 17.5 mm calibre and 146.5 cm in overall length. It has a reputation for being inferior to the Bess but its performance was always impaired by inferior powder.

The British soldier's principle weapon was a variation of the famous .75 in cal. Brown Bess smooth-bore musket that had been in army service use

The Volley Gun was designed by Capt James Wilson and originally conceived as a defence weapon for ship's officers. The specification was to pierce a 3 in hole to a depth of six men. Six barrels were brazed to a central seventh barrel, which was fitted with a 'Nock' patent breech. The flintlock ignition fired through the pan to the chamber directly beneath. All seven barrels fired simultaneously, each loaded with a pistol charge – 2 drams of powder and a .52 calibre lead ball. The gun weighed over 14 lb. It became an offensive weapon at sea, but was thought too hazardous, endangering the rigging and sails with flames from the ignition. Rifleman Moore of the 95th Rifles, who owns the gun, is seen here and attests to the tremendous destructive power after his trials with it in the Crimea

from 1720. The most common version was the Short Land Pattern with its 42 in (106.7 cm) barrel that was issued in 1768, although the cheaper India Pattern, which was slightly shorter still, was gradually coming in as a replacement from 1793.

Rifles: Britain was probably the only nation to equip a significant number of its men with rifles. Other armies had them, especially among their jager or chasseur corps but the 60th and 95th regiments became something of a legend with their accurate shooting. These élite troops were issued with a Baker rifle. the inside of the barrel was not smooth but grooved in a spiral, which imparted spin to the ball as it travelled up its length. This meant that the ball did not take the deflection of the last barrel bounce so dramatically and the grooves also sent it spiralling through the air, equalising any shape or weight defect in the ball and giving it a balanced flight. Both these factors greatly improved the accuracy and the range of the firearm. It was not unknown for a marksman noted for his expertise (such as Plunkett at Cacabelos) to make shot at 300 yd, although this was a great exception. The Baker rifle was not a truly accurate arm, but the use of a greased patch to get a better fit between ball and bore, as well as training in the 'tactical rifle system' and line firing, made it a fearsome one.

Bayonets: By the 1800s, armies had gone over to socket bayonets, which were a considerable improvement upon the old-fashioned plug types because, even when fixed, they permitted the musket to be loaded and fired. The socket is a metal tube that fits over the barrel and locks manually in place by means of a zigzag slot. There were many varieties of socket, including the split, which catered for use with different sized barrels. Some had clips, some springs and the Swedes adopted a wing nut version. The French used a rotating ring to close the slot while the British had the simple, cheap manual type. The blade, extending from the socket, was offset to the right of the barrel. It was offset so that it was not in the way of the shot and so that the soldier's hand was clear of its edge when he rammed home. It was not on top as this would impede even rudimentary sighting, nor was it below because the ramrod had to be drawn from its pipe easily. Soldiers' tales tell why right was preferred over left, but the locking catch was then on the top so the men could see it.

Blades varied in length and shape. The longest and thinnest was possibly the 1784 spear bayonet for Egg's Carbine, which was nearly 40 in or 100 cm long and was designed to be used as a spear. The length supposedly compensated for the short barrel of the cavalryman's firearm. The first common style was the two-edged flat variety but, although made of steel, it was prone to buckling and twisting, so most nations adopted a triangular cross-section to impart strength and rigidity. British troops were reputedly 'fond' of using the 'pricker'; and their triangular Brown Bess bayonets were around 45 cm long (including socket) and had 35 cm blades (French: 40 cm)

THE SOLDIER'S WEAPON

Initially, the soldier tends to think his weapon is his only defence against his enemy. As he becomes accustomed to using it, especially in action, he usually comes around to regard it as an offensive arm, and later still as a 'friend or companion'. Musket and rifle care was drilled into the recruit; if it malfunctioned it became an expensive club. He had to learn how to dismantle and clean it thoroughly, how to replace or mend any basic pieces and to reassemble it. In particular, setting a flint was a skill, and one that had to be performed in the heat of battle. Burnt blackpowder left a residue that built up and fouled the pan, clogging the touch-hole and filling the chamber which had to be washed out with boiling water. In battle the men urinated down the barrels, the hot metal boiling the urine, which proved chemically more effective than H_2O. Against regulations, men also personalised their guns with brass butt plates or brass nails, and inscribed stock plaques became an official way of bestowing an honour or reward. Some weapons had pet names, such as Crockett's famous 'Betsy', while a whole make was named the 'Brown Bess' and the Chassepot was referred to as the 'Chasseur' by the French and the 'chase pot' or the 'piss pot' by the British.

RIFLEMAN MOORE OF THE
95TH RIFLES DEMONSTRATING
HOW TO PREPARE AND FIRE
THE BAKER RIFLE USING A
CARTRIDGE

1. 'Opening' lock ready for loading. Some Riflemen carried a feather or small copper pick in the vent when the rifle was loaded – this made for a safer operating procedure when replacing the priming in the pan

2. To charge the rifle, the Rifleman first draws a cartridge from his pouch . . .

3. . . . biting off the paper containing the ball or cutting the cartridge across the sharp gunflint

4. The barrel is then charged with powder from the measured amount contained within the cartridge

5. The empty cartridge is then discarded and the ball – ready wrapped in its greased leather patch –

6. . . . is pushed into the rifle barrel

7. The flat end of the ramrod is used to 'start' the ball into the bore

8. The bullet is then slowly pushed down to the powder using the ramrod

9. The ramrod is replaced below the barrel

10. The lock is primed using the pinch of 'fine' powder from the cow horn flask

11. The lock is closed

12. The Rifleman adjusts for target and range – early rifles did have a variable sight for elevation – then takes careful aim

13. The Baker rifle is well capable of hitting man-sized targets at up to 250 yd, although greater ranges are possible through practice and using the 'prone' and 'orthodox' positions when aiming

14. Two original 'patched' balls, an unpatched ball and exact replicas of two cartridges constructed by Rifleman Moore

Note: a separate 'charger' is attached to Rifleman Moore's powder horn. This was used in various forms by many riflemen to charge the rifle with their 'own' powder measure from the horn for consistent shooting, avoiding the spillage from tearing cartridges – the service charge for the Baker was 4½ drams of gunpowder – and it can shoot accurately on a battlefield with half that amount – also avoiding the excessive recoil that the service charge creates. The brass powder horn top was notorious for getting lost or broken on campaign, many of them being 'fixed' by the soldiers by stopping up the aperture with a bottle cork.

Text copyright R. R-Moore, 1985. Excerpts from original source material in 'Practical Experiments in ascertaining the Battlefield Effectiveness of the Flintlock Musket and Rifle 1808–1815 Part II' – 'Application' and 'Recreating the 95th Rifleman at War, 1808–1815' with hollow-ground fullers on the reverse, thus making them lighter and easier to wield accurately. Again, the myth of letting the blood run out is a bit far-fetched, although twisting and extracting a fullered blade was a much easier task than using the non-fuller type. They still bent and diaries tell of men hammering their bayonets out straight again after battle. Riflemen were issued with a sword bayonet, that is, it doubled in function as both a hand-held and a firearm-fixed weapon. Some had serrated back edges, which meant it could also be used as a saw. Apart from fighting, the 'pricker' was a favourite implement for cooking, loop-holing, digging and threatening civilians.

Artillery: Artillery manufacture still employed the established practices of the past 300 years. The metal barrels were cast from various amalgams of bronze, iron or brass. Bronze resists corrosion better than iron and it can withstand greater pressures without cracking. Improvements centred around the development of the poundage system and universal agreement on calibres and weight of shot in respect to charge. Innovations came in the design of the carriages and the limber systems used to draw them, especially in France, with the universal redesigning work of Gribeauval. By Napoleon's rise, artillery had divided into guns and howitzers. Howitzers evolved from the need to lob bombs into defensive works but they had other advantages too, such as high trajectory shell throwing that, with a well-timed or cut fuse, could explode above a formation of troops. However, the principal advantage was that the howitzer was lighter than the gun, 275 lb between comparative 12-pdrs. It also needed less propellant. Its disadvantages were that it could not fire so heavy a missile and its range was some 600 yd shorter.

Different ranges were still achieved by varying the angle of elevation. These were approximately:

Gun	1°	2°	3°	5°	10°
3-pdr	700 yd	950 yd	1,150 yd	1,400 yd	2,390 yd
60-pdr	750	1,050	1,310	1,800	2,800
12-pdr	800	1,150	1,450	1,900	3,200

and their 'calculated average' casualty damage factors on a column would be:

Gun	400 yd	800 yd	1,200 yd
3-pdr	30 men	19 men	4 men
6-pdr	39	28	8
120-pdr	48	36	12

For cavalry and skirmishers halve the totals and quarter them for deployed skirmishers or gun crews in action.

A typical 12-pdr field gun needed quite a team of men and horses to get it into action. Usually there were 8 gunners, 5 working the gun directly with 3 serving ammunition. Both the limber and the ammunition caisson took 6 horses with 3 drivers. So a British battery of 6 guns or a French of 8 required a minimum of 84 or 112 men and 72 or 96 horses. Add the senior officers and supernumeries and it became a formation that required quite a logistic exercise to fight. Crews could work with fewer men as casualties occurred and the drivers could be drawn upon, although this was of little use when they were untrained twelve-year-old plough-boys as many of the French drivers were at Waterloo.

Above, right: Royal Cypher on the top of a naval cannon

'The devil's own artillery' were inaccurate and unreliable but had a demoralising effect on the enemy as they cut a swathe through the ranks in a haphazard fashion, picking off individuals seemingly with a will of their own

British Royal Horse Artillery

THE WAR AT SEA

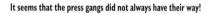

Whitehall, July 9, 1803.

Whereas the Lords Commissioners of the Admiralty have represented to His Majesty, that, in the Evening of Saturday last, the 2d Instant, Lieutenant Fullarton and Lieutenant Palmer, of His Majesty's Ship Squirrel, having been sent on Shore from the said Ship, then lying in the River Thames, with the Boat-swain, Gunner, several Petty Officers, and a Party of Twenty-five Men, in Quest of some Seamen, of whom Captain Losack, the Commander of the said Ship, had received Information; and having landed at the Village of Barking, in the County of Essex, about Nine o'Clock in the Evening, and impressed Four Seamen for His Majesty's Service, several evil disposed Persons assembled near the said Village, attacked the said Lieutenant and their Party, and rescued the said Seamen; and that afterwards, on the Parties' Return to the River Side, in order to go on board their Ship, they were met and opposed by a very numerous Body of Haymakers and others, to the Number of Five Hundred and upwards, armed with Sabres, Pitchforks, and other offensive Weapons, by whom they were attacked and assaulted in a most violent and cruel Manner, and particularly Lieutenant Palmer received Two very severe Wounds in different Parts of his Body, and is now lying at Barking in imminent Danger of his Life;

His Majesty, for the better discovering the Offenders concerned in the abovementioned violent Outrages and Assaults, and bringing them to Justice, is hereby pleased to offer His most gracious Pardon to any One or more of them; (except such of them as actually wounded the said Lieutenant Palmer, or any of the Party with him,) who shall apprehend, or give such Information as shall be the Means of apprehending any of his Accomplices.

PELHAM.

It seems that the press gangs did not always have their way!

For many, the seafaring life started as a brawl as the press gang ranged through the inns and villages countrywide

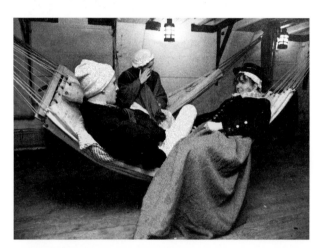

'Docksies' were allowed on board ship while in port

Food varied from ship to ship. Here is one menu recorded from the time: Breakfast – burgoo (made from coarse oatmeal and water); Scotch coffee (a mixture of burnt bread boiled in water and sweetened with sugar); Noon – grog ration, 1 gill of rum and 3 of water sweetened with sugar or flavoured with lemon; Supper – biscuit, cheese and butter. Nelson insisted that the men on his fleet be given onions or fruit to prevent the disease known as scurvy – caused by a lack of vitamin C

For the few hours available when not working, sailors would play cards or dice, or carve intricate models of ships from bone or wood

The midshipman was a junior or trainee officer

The Royal Marines, Per Mare, Per Terram. Permanent divisions were raised in 1755 with the origins of the Corps going back to 1664. These men were the marine infantry, often landing from small boats to storm outposts of Napoleon's army. The Emperor, after his defeat, commented, 'Much might be done with a hundred thousand men such as these'

Discipline was harsh, but was expected by the men to be so. A Cat O' Nine Tails – or whip – would reduce a man's back to shreds, often exposing the bone

At sea, or in fortifications, far heavier guns were employed as they did not need to be dragged around by horses. They remained in position and the attacking enemy came to them. On land, complicated overlapping fields of fire were worked out to maximise the effect of static pieces, but at sea the fighting platform itself, that is, the ship, manoeuvred into position. Ships were floating gun batteries, some with up to three extensive platforms or decks mounted one over the other, each with its guns protruding from square 'portholes' along its sides. Each gun had a limited traverse in the broadside and it was up to those sailing the vessel to bring her into a position to maximise all her guns. Each type of gun aboard a ship had a purpose and this was sometimes enhanced by the type of projectile they fired. The really heavy guns were the 32-pdrs, whose round shot smashed an enemy's wooden walls and penetrated the hull, disabling guns and showering the guncrews with flying slivers of timber. Catching a wooden ship as she rolled up, a skilled gunner could hole her beneath the waterline and cause immense problems. The 24-pdrs did a similar job but were employed usually against the superstructure and the thinner walls of the upper decks, while the 12-pdrs were used to fire chain or bar shot and chop the rigging to pieces, making the ship lose speed and become difficult to control. Gradually she would become impossible to manoeuvre and prone to stem and stern rakes that could strip out men and guns the length of a deck. Carronades were short, large-bore guns that were employed as men-killers on the upper decks; packed with musket balls or stones and 'hard waste' they were deck-clearers at short range. (Text continues on p. 48)

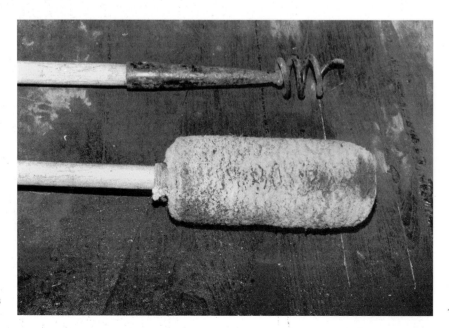

Above: worm used to remove debris from cannon; below: sponge used to cool barrel after each firing and put out smouldering remnants of charge to prevent premature ignition when the next charge is inserted

The worm is put down the barrel to pull out the debris

The wet sponge cools the inside of the barrel

The flannel bag holding a measured charge of
gunpowder is inserted

Chainshot is selected – two cannon balls joined by
heavy chain (note the quoits to prevent the cannon
balls rolling about the deck)

The chainshot is loaded

Wadding follows

The propellant and projectiles are rammed home

The cannon is run out

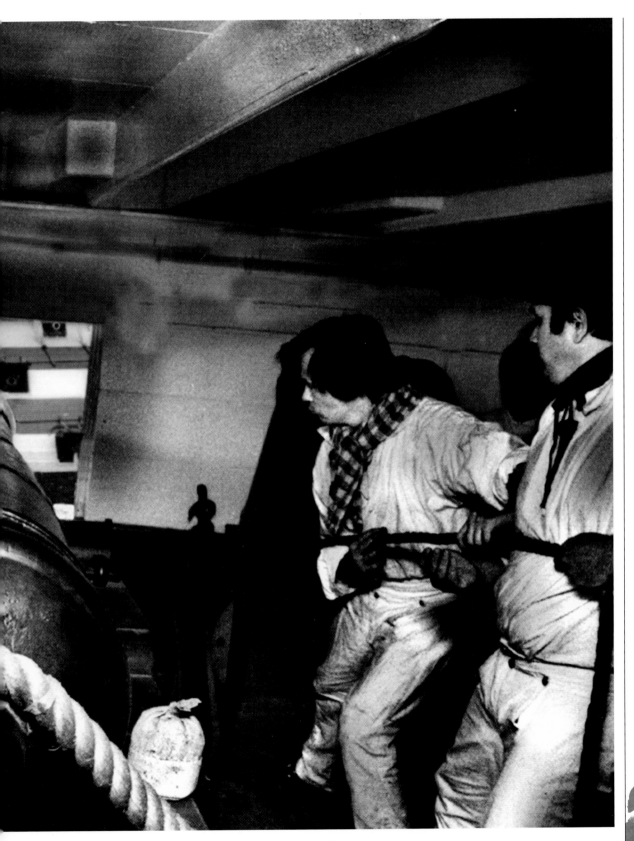

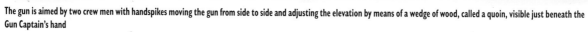

The gun is aimed by two crew men with handspikes moving the gun from side to side and adjusting the elevation by means of a wedge of wood, called a quoin, visible just beneath the Gun Captain's hand

Waiting for the right moment. The priming powder is lit by the Gun Captain, who stays out of the range of recoil

The tube of powder ignites and fires the main charge, propelling the iron projectile with awesome force. The gun recoils to the extent of the heavy ropes threaded through the rear of

the cannon breach

The process is started all over again. Discipline and, to some extent, superior gun powder made the Royal Navy a deadly efficient adversary once the enemy ship was at close quarters

No hesitation in reloading, but an ominous silence comes from the French ship – a broadside is coming

The air is thick with sulphurous smoke and screams of agony. The young Powder Monkey, already wounded an hour before, suffers a mortal wound

As the gun crews recover and return fire, Royal Marine snipers on the deck are shooting at the French Officers om the quarterdeck while musket balls hiss past them and chainshot rips through the rigging

The wounded are taken down to the cockpit for the surgeon

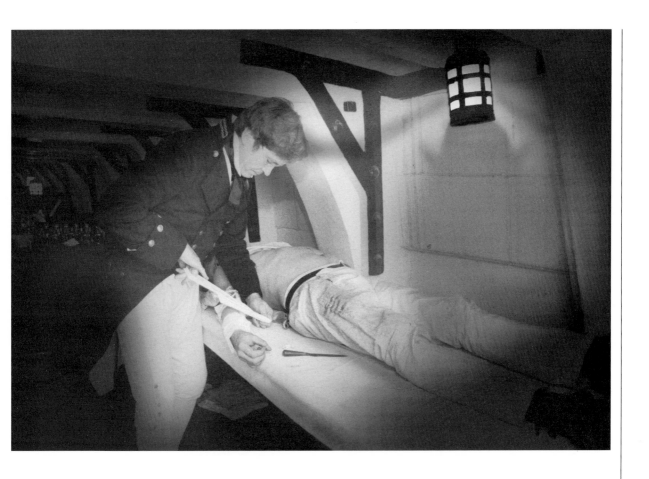

The surgeon generally worked below the waterline on the Orlop deck and so was relatively safe from the carnage taking place a few feet above his head

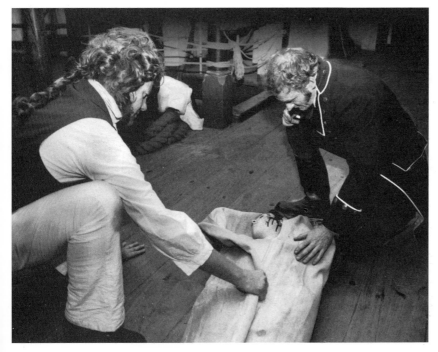

After victory or defeat, the dead are buried at sea, sewn into their own hammocks and weighted with a cannon ball

45

1.

2.

5.

6.

9.

10.

ROYAL MARINE MUSKET DRILL

3.

4.

7.

8.

11.

The curved wide blade used by the light cavalry was swished down in an arc, ideal for cutting down fleeing infantry

Swords, Sabres and Lances: There were national differences in all swords and sabres but, generally speaking, there were two distinct types of swords, one for infantry officers and the other for artillerymen, and two distinct types of sabres, one for the heavy cavalry and one for the light cavalry. The infantry officer's sword was not really a fighting weapon, more a badge of rank. It was straight and designed for thrusting or, indeed, pointing in a chosen direction. Some junior officers carried swords of inferior quality that broke easily, although the general thinness of the pattern did not prevent this happening to better blades when fending off cavalry or blocking a swipe from a gunner's spike. Artillery were issued with short swords similar to the classical Roman gladius but they were often of such poor quality as to be useless, except for chopping wood, so the men preferred to fight with the implements of their trade – the handspikes, the ramrods and porte-feus.

The heavy cavalry sabre was long and straight and used for thrusting. It had a sharpened point with a back edge to the top 6 inches. They were often weighty, blade-heavy, clumsy and difficult to use. The idea of placing the point just to the side of a cuirass and thrusting in under the armpit as opposing lines met at a canter was an elusive dream. More usual was the crash of horseflesh followed by a protracted close fight as the men used the chop and hack coupled with the guard-punch. Their target was more often than not their enemy's mount, which, if felled, took its rider out of the fray as well. The light cavalry used a curve-bladed slicing weapon. It had a flat, wide blade and was swished down in an arc. Their design was based upon the swords carried by horsemen from the eastern and Arab nations, such as the Hungarian Hussars and the Mamelukes. They were ideal for cutting down fleeing infantry.

Despite its pedigree, the lance was a relative newcomer to warfare. It went out of fashion after the decline of the mounted knight and it took the reorganised French army to restore its popularity. Nearly 3 m long, its ash shaft was tipped with a leaf-bladed, hollow-ground point, roughly rectangular in cross-section and socketed onto the shaft. Lancer regiments used them in the first impact to skewer the enemy before they could get in close enough to use the sabre. However, once that first clash was over they were a liability as the press made them difficult to use. Even lancer regiments restricted their use to front rank troops only, the second rank charging with drawn sabres. The lance came into its own against disordered bodies, and lancers were effective in riding down broken infantry or scattered cavalry. The destruction of the Union Brigade at Waterloo has been accredited to the reach of the lancer, especially from behind. It could be thrust into the back, twisted and dragged free by the transferred impetus of the horse transmitted through the leather wrist strap.

A Polish Lancer of the 1st Regiment Polish Lancers

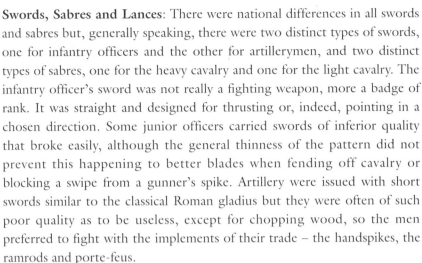

THEIR FIGHTING

The early years of the Revolutionary Wars gave rise to the undisciplined mass attack in depth. The General officers threw large numbers of untrained citizen-soldiers at specific points in the enemy line in the hope that their numbers and *élan* would swamp, overrun and break their foes. At times it worked, but more usually they were shot down by the well-drilled regulars they faced. It was Minister for War Carnot who reorganised and reformed the French army. He welded the old royal regulars and the new *levées* into more equal fighting units and gave them new identities not associated with past defeats or historic myths linked to aristocrat officers. Nicknamed the 'Organiser of Victory', Carnot advocated the strategy of manoeuvre and the tactics of mobility, with the selective application of hard pressure, that were to enable Napoleon to conquer most of Europe. The rise of Napoleon was not due to the fact that he applied a dramatically different set of principles to war, but that he moved quickly, paid little heed to protecting his communications, took chances and was always ready to fight – the direct antithesis to the hidebound eighteenth-century mentality of his adversaries. Few of his moves or systems were new; only the speed and efficiency at which they were performed made them appear radical. Audacious strategy could only operate with properly organised, well-equipped and well-run armies and it was the organisational genius and administrative skills of Carnot, the inventiveness of Gribeauval, coupled with the driving, powerful will of Napoleon and the patriotic fervour of the ordinary French soldiers, that won the War of the First Coalition.

The revolutionary forces had produced a new idea – that of men advancing at their own speed in a clump rather than a straight line. This was formalised under Napoleon into the famous column of attack, and then improved upon with 'clouds' of skirmishers preceding it. These tactics suited the French Army, whose emphasis upon drillbook training was never as great as the Allies. Conscripts could be inspired, cajoled or forced forward by putting them in the middle of a huge block of men, the momentum of the body carrying them along. All they had to do was march at the enemy, sing and shout a lot, and rely upon the veteran companies to shoot off the head of the column or go in with the bayonet. There were different formations, including the *ordre mixte* of two battalion columns linked by a battalion line that combined the firepower of the line with the mêlée impact of the column, but they required trained men to perform them. As casualty rates, disease and desertion stripped out these men, the less complicated, bludgeoning column became the more usual mode of attack.

The backbone of any army was the standard infantryman – abbreviated colloquially to the PBI, or Poor Bloody Infantry – whose task it was to take and hold ground. They were, by the nature of their muskets, used en masse in close formations and fired volleys by section, division, platoon, company or rank. It was their duty to move or stand where they were told, usually

49

Close quarters hack and slash of the cavalry mêlée

shoulder to shoulder, and, disdaining cover, trade fire with their opposite numbers. However, most European armies had learnt the value of light infantry from the American campaigns and had 'light companies' in each of their regiments who could supposedly skirmish and then retire into the line. The French developed the idea by creating special regiments who could perform either role, and this *infanterie légère* would swarm forward in open order, annoy and disrupt a line, while screening the advance of an attacking 'heavy' column. Wellington employed thick skirmish screens to protect his line – so thick they were, at times, mistaken for a first line. Other nations responded with their own light infantry and some went even further by raising special units from gamekeepers, hunters and men with an independent disposition; these were the 'jagers'. They were trained

Each British battalion had a squad of pioneers. They cut down enemy barricades and built defences. This pioneer is armed with a flintlock Musketoon.

Infantrymen of the 42nd Royal Highland Regiment

skirmishers – sharpshooters selecting targets and shooting as individuals. There were never many of them, although the idea caught on in Britain where the 60th and the 95th were armed with rifles. The fostering of a regular élite rifle body was not popular with the French authorities, although their men who fought in this manner often sought a prized Baker trophy.

Being a barn-door weapon the smooth-bore musket had to be used in numbers to make an impression and the best way to do this was to adopt a formation that maximised the number of men capable of firing at any one time. This was the line, the favoured tactic of the eighteenth century and the established way of fighting. Most countries had their lines three ranks deep, the first two fired while the third retained its fire to counter any emergency that might arise. On some occasions the second and third ranks harrowed across the gaps to fire a full volley. This could be disastrous for new recruits, such as the Maria-Louise conscripts who supposedly did more damage to their own front ranks than to the enemy.

The line was the formation that could deliver the maximum firepower of a battalion. Its fire was often devastating but national methods of deployment produced tactical differences. The French stood in three ranks and fired in one massed volley. However, the third rank was hindered by the first two and the men generally fired high. Thus a French battalion of 600 men in three ranks lost about 33 per cent of its firepower. Although regulations still specified that the firing line was to be in three ranks, the British field practice was to stand in two ranks and fire rolling volleys by divisions. Consequently, all 1,000 men in a battalion fired reasonably effectively – even when two French battalions, 1,200 men, traded shot with one British regiment they really only got off 800 or so effective rounds to the British 1,000. When single battalions went up against each other, as was common practice, they were seriously outgunned. The line was the perfect answer to attacking infantry but, the soldiers being thinly spread, it was an easy target for cavalry, especially from the flanks, from where a charge could roll up the entire formation.

Infantry tried to meet cavalry in square, an all-round defensive formation, a minimum of four men deep and bristling with a hedge of bayonets, into which a horse was extremely unlikely to go. The men had to be well trained and show great resolution to stand their ground when the heavy cavalry thundered towards them (the Russian Army extras filming 'Waterloo' broke several times), but if they stood, and the rear ranks poured fire into the horsemen, the rearless and flankless square usually protected them. However, artillery could seriously damage this densely packed formation and the tactic was for the cavalry to be accompanied in attack by their horse artillery, who would gallop up, unlimber and pound it until it broke, thus allowing the cavalry to charge down the fleeing men.

Cavalry usually attacked in separate squadrons in three waves. They did it in various formations, in line of regiments, checkerboard of squadrons or

Sabre and sabretasche

Light Cavalry attack

echelon of squadrons, but the principle was the same. The first to go in did so at the full gallop to minimise time spent under fire. They were the assault troops and they had only to break into the enemy and disrupt them. The second wave, the support troops, about 300 yd behind, then pushed open and widened the break the first line had made and cleared the gap. The third wave covered the flank of the first two during their advance and then went through the cleared gap to exploit the situation, turning left and right by troops, surrounding disordered men and cutting them down. If a fourth squadron was present it was the reserve and covered the other flank. Assault, break and exploit became the principal tactic of most attacks and was the premise upon which the Somme and D-Day battles were fought.

It happened too on a grand scale with the French infantry, with a Corps attack being in three divisions and a reserve. However, the men's perception was limited to what happened immediately around them. Moving in line was difficult, so they were formed into columns of regiments, each battalion usually two companies wide and three companies deep and then the rest of the regiment similarly arrayed behind (theoretically 60 men wide × 27 or more deep). Depending on the size of the attack, the ground and the composition of the division, three regimental columns would be placed side by side, with the fourth dispersed as a 'cloud' of skirmishers across the whole front. With officers etc., around 7,500 men were densely packed together in a deep clump on a frontage of 150 yd allowing for inter-regimental spaces. It was a superb hammer, and the men needed very little training to do it. There were variations of course: the centre regiment could be in line to provide covering fire power (*l'ordre mixte*), the fourth could act as another column instead of light infantry, or the regiments could double up, reducing the frontage to less than 100 yd.

Ier Regiment de Chasseurs à Cheval de Ligne Ier Escadron

On the battlefield, the tactic was simple. Napoleon used his guns massed in a grand battery, usually on high ground, to bombard the enemy formations before his columns advanced. Although discouraged for obvious reasons, skilled gunners could use the height to keep the gun firing over the heads of their own men until they nearly reached the enemy line. Thus, field artillery would bombard the enemy to 'soften them up', while the columns were set in motion. As these dense formations got to within 250 yd the heavy guns would cease and their own regimental light artillery or accompanying horse artillery would give local close-proximity fire support. Their skirmishers would begin sporadic musketry that grew in intensity the nearer they got. At 100 yd the head of the columns might fire on the move and then the *pas de charge* would increase the speed, causing the whole mass to lurch forward with bayonets gleaming. Absorbing the skirmishers, the attack pressed home over the last 20 yd at the charge. Frequently, the enemy were not inclined to stay; they broke and ran away.

Opposite: top row and centre row: Military routine on campaign. The 12th Light Dragoon Cavalry; bottom row, left: Demonstration of the effectiveness of horse and sabre; bottom row, right: The British Hussar (Light Cavalry)

However, the column was also a superb target and the British Army learnt quickly how to counter it. Wellington deployed his defending line infantry on a reverse slope to protect it from the enemy guns. He put his own guns in pairs along the crest and threw forward two screens of skirmishers of his own: the first being companies of élite light infantry and/or riflemen 300 yd forward of the crest, and the second being the light companies of the line regiments 250 yd forward. The scenario above becomes:

French guns do the skirmishers in extended and open order very little harm and do not touch the main force. At 1,000 yards from the crest the column starts being hit and the men smashed by roundshot. At 75 paces to the minute they take this for 5½ minutes seeing their comrades drop and closing the gaps with the casualty rates getting higher and higher. With 600 yards to go the skirmisher officers begin to fall to the marksmen and by 300 the skirmishers have been neutralised by a firefight with both lines. Men start slipping away from the rear of the column. Seeing the British retire, new heart enters the men and they press foward, only to be cut down in swathes by canister and the line officers get the riflemen's attention. The British line crests the hill and aims, the light companies retire. With just 100 yards to go to the crest, the shattered front ranks try to fire but infilling and lack of officers make it a sporadic and ineffective affair. More men drop off the rear. As the 'doublir' to 120 paces to the minute is sounded, the British muskets begin their volleying by divisions in a constant storm of ball interrupted only by the crash of more canister. French casualties are enormous and the column begins to fall into confusion as the rear pushes forward and the front recoils. The British volleys continue, and the rear of the column, stepping over the dead, loses heart and even more men run away. The confused mass comes on, taking more and more losses, to about 20 yards when the British line falls momentarily silent before it delivers a full battalion volley and the guns belch grape which together mow down ranks and chop wedges out of the formation. The rear companies run. The British give their infamous 'great shout', level bayonets and surge forward. Fear and panic overtakes the remaining French and they quickly join their comrades fleeing to the rear, slipping on the blood and slithering down the hill. The attack has resulted in the deaths of hundreds and the destruction of the regiment for very little loss inflicted.

This is a simplified and perhaps romanticised view but it epitomises what came to be referred to as: 'they came on in the old manner and we saw them off in the same old style.'

THE AMERICAN CIVIL WAR

THE AMERICAN CIVIL WAR

After the war of 1812, America underwent a change, turned her back upon Europe and focussed inward and westward. Old ties with Britain were broken, the Canadian boundaries were agreed, Spain finally gave up Florida, and the famous Monroe Doctrine evolved. Immigration and western expansion meant America grew rapidly in population and area, and this shifted the centre of power. Indians east of the Mississippi were ejected as punishment for their British war alliance and the fertile country of the South became home to settlers who could farm on an industrial scale, especially cotton. In the North the rich, open territories

below the Great Lakes also acquired vast numbers of settler communities. The eastern seaboard states found their old supremacy challenged by their new western neighbours, whose insistence upon democratic processes threatened the establishment and the ruling class. Their growing numbers also threatened to swamp national representation. The East disliked the new money of the plantation owners and feared for their cheap factory labour, lured west by the adventure of pioneering. In turn, the western states resented the economic power of the moneyed east; old rivalries gave way to sectional interests.

By 1830 new rivals for political power had arisen. Andrew Jackson held the West with a party founded upon strict democratic principles and opposition to eastern big-money corruption. John Quincy Adams rallied the East for those who rejected majority rule and resented the power being amassed by frontier dirt-scratchers. Jackson, 'the Tennessee brawler', and the Democrats won a resounding election victory and dismantled the bigoted civil service, removing large-scale corruption but absorbing many state indiosyncrasies into the Federal machine. Throughout the next twenty-five years the western expansion continued. Facilitated by new waves of immigration and the development of the railway network, more states joined the Union. The political need to balance individual state and Federal interests centred on two main issues: the supremacy of the Union and the organisation of a national economy. North and South split over protectionism and trade tariffs. North and West split over interest rates, while West and South were at odds over support for the war with Mexico. Into this internecine struggle of factions and alliances came the moral and financial issue of slavery. South of the 40th parallel the economy was based upon an agricultural, labour-intensive slave system denied to the industrial

North and irrelevant to the new territories of the West. Slave owners controlled the Republican politics of the southern seaboard. Northern protectionist politicians saw an opportunity to create alliances with the democratic western states north of the 40th and the champions of democratic freedom in the new west coast territories so as to undermine the power of the old South. Mobilising a hitherto disinterested public, nineteenth-century Christianity turned its scandalised glare on the South and challenged its very foundations. Of the 6,000,000 white inhabitants of the 'slave states' only about 3,000 were principal slave owners; however, there were 300,000 lesser slave owners, 1,000,000 farmers and enough 'mean whites' to forge an army.

The division became exaggerated by social differences. The southern, landed aristocracy looked down upon the factory-owning northerners with old-world distaste for 'trade' and vulgar commercialism, while the more puritan-biased North censured the indolence and hedonistic lifestyle of the southern gentry. The rift, when it came, was political and constitutional – the North upholding the notion of federalism and the South proclaiming state sovereign rights. Secessionists held that as states had voluntarily joined the Union for common benefits, they had the democratic right to leave it if they felt that belonging impaired their sovereignty and economic and social stability. Federalists maintained the Union was indivisible, an agreed entity enshrined in a national consciousness. The vehicle for this struggle was slavery and the complex constitutional arguments surrounding it and its extension into the new territories. Political, regional, economic, social and moral passions rose. Tempers flared, violent incidents occurred and an 1860 election returned Abraham Lincoln, the northern Democrat and anti-slaver, as President Elect. Slavery would not be permitted in the West and the balance of power would swing irrevocably north. South Carolina quit the Union, quickly followed by Mississippi, Florida, Alabama, Georgia, Louisiana and Texas. Delegates of these seceding states organised themselves into a Confederacy and elected Jefferson Davis as President, with a mandate to raise 100,000 men for an army.

Lincoln swore to maintain the property of the US national government in the South and ordered the resupply of Fort Sumter at the mouth of the Charleston harbour in South Carolina. Davis ordered General Beauregard to secure Sumter. After two days of bombardment the garrison capitulated and marched out unscathed. However, the twenty-three free states of the North interpreted the bombardment as an act of aggression and banded together. Lincoln called up 75,000 of the northern militias to suppress the seven rebellious states. The war had begun.

Voting to reject Lincoln's right to use force to coerce membership of the Union, Virginia joined the Confederacy and so did Arkansas, Tennessee, and North Carolina. The border slave states, Kentucky, Missouri, Maryland and Delaware, all tried to secede but political and military action kept them officially in the Union although in reality their manpower fought on both

A WAR OF FIRSTS

Some of the many innovations in use during the American Civil War:

- Submarines
- Aerial reconnaissance by balloon
- Repeating rifles
- Telescopic sights
- Steel ships
- Machine-guns
- Anaesthetics for wounded
- Naval torpedoes
- Railroad artillery
- Trench systems
- Naval camouflage – as used by the rust-grey blockade runners
- First economic war – North floods South with counterfeit money

sides. Virginia split too as, encouraged by her neighbour Ohio, the west of the state seceded from the Secession.

The war lasted from 1861 to 1865 and ranged across America from the Atlantic to the Pacific, although its principal attention and action was focussed in the more inhabited and strategically important areas. The highest concentrations of actions were fought in Maryland and Virginia in the east and Tennessee and Mississippi in the west, although North Georgia was heavily fought over too. It was a war of rapid movement and stalemated fortified lines; of lightning raids and protracted sieges; of dramatic charges and withering crossfires; of factory production lines and handmade hunting rifles. Rapid progress in understanding the potential of technology also made it a war of 'firsts'. Weapon manufacturers developed the first practical machine-gun, railway-mounted mobile siege artillery, widespread use of land mines, submarines, torpedoes, and the mass production of repeating rifles. Civil engineers enabled the first extensive use of field trenches, railway troop transport, balloon reconnaissance, combat photography and field telegraphs. Centralised services created the first hospital trains, black US battalions, field elections, and America's first taste of the draft and income tax. The war had its much darker 'firsts' as well, with racist and hate propaganda filling newspapers; war correspondents' lurid tales; casualty bulletin boards; massive civilian displacement; policies of total war; deliberate large-scale destruction of civil property; starvation camps; and the eradication of a culture and a way of life – ethnic cleansing. To all intents and purposes, the American Civil War was the first modern war.

THE MEN

At the outbreak of the war the only regular force was a small Union Army of about 16,000 men. With the Secession, 313 professional officers and 26 other ranks resigned their commissions and allegiances to take up commands and posts in the rapidly organised Army of the Confederacy. Davis's February mandate to raise 100,000 volunteers had 35,000 under arms by mid-April 1861, thus outnumbering the Union 2:1. Lincoln's reply was to call upon the northern militias for 75,000 men. By July '61 McDowell lead 2,000 regulars and 36,000 volunteers against Beauregard's 20,000 at Bull Run (see pp. 62–3, only to find Johnson's 12,000 reinforcements had arrived and he had conceived a plan too complicated for his men to execute. These were the men of the first engagements. The majority were raw recruits with little training and poor understanding of military demands. As the war moved from its early months, many of those volunteers grew more and more accustomed to the trade and evolved into regulars, although some units were blessed or cursed with a continuing 'irregular attitude' to drill, orders and discipline. Likewise as the months turned to years, those who survived became veterans. Boys who lied about

Boys who had lied about their age in 1861 were hard-bitten, grim, veteran soldiers by the time of their eighteenth birthdays in '65

their ages in 1861 were hard-bitten, grim veteran soldiers by their eighteenth birthdays in '65. For all this, the average infantryman drew $13 a month, the purchase cost of his rifle. In the early stages of the conflict the only men who had received military training, apart from the small US regular army, were the various state, county or city militias. These became the core of early regiments of both North and South. Militia units were built up in strength and some, like the 14th Brooklyn, served all the way through the war, although they were renamed the 84th New York. Most regiments took anyone who came forward but some units recruited only certain types of volunteers; 'Ellsworth's Avengers' only enlisted unmarried, fit men of good character and high intelligence who were in their twenties and over 5 ft 9 in tall. They served as the 44th New York.

The Confederacy called upon a country population brought up with horses and consequently had a far superior cavalry arm at their disposal. Romantic notions of chivalry also encouraged young Southerners gallantly to ride off to war rather than walk. The North had farm boys, but the economy was dependent upon drag horses rather than herders and bloodstock. Quite possibly, it did not occur to a northern ploughboy or factory worker that he could acquire military status and social prestige simply by getting on a horse's back – looking after a horse was hard work so

Immigrant communities formed their own battalions and often dressed in a style reminiscent of their homeland, such as these French-style Zouaves

THE FIRST BATTLE
OF BULL RUN

1. Above: 20 July 1861. Both sides prepare for imminent battle
2. Right: Evening – The 'Ominous Stillness'

5. The Confederate rebels hold their position

6. Despite a fierce attack by the Union forces, the position is held until 12 noon

9. At around 1400 hrs, Union forces under McDowell advance on the Confederate position

10. The Union advance is thrown back

3. Dawn, 21 July 1861

4. The Northern Artillery had opened fire at 0500. The Confederates learn of the Union advance, and meet them as they approach from Sudley Ford

7. Left: Confederates then fall back to Henry House Hill
8. Above: Because of the stout defence of their position by Evans, Jackson and others at a critical time, Jackson will get the nickname 'Stonewall'

11. Above: The main road of retreat is blocked and the Rebels celebrate their first victory
12. Right: The Rebels list 387 dead, 1,582 wounded. The Union lose 460 men, with 1,124 injured, and 1,312 listed as missing

he generally joined the infantry. We have records for the Union that show that of the 2,300,000 men who enlisted, 70 per cent were under twenty-three years old. Many of those were younger still: 200,000 were fifteen or sixteen, 300 were between eleven and fourteen, and 25 were ten years old.

The first black troops of the Civil War were volunteers formed into the 1st South Carolina Regiment, later called the 33rd Regiment US Coloured Troops. Some 186,000 black soldiers served in the Union Army and did much to further the truth of racial equality although they often suffered abuse from their own so-called comrades in arms and frequently were issued inferior equipment and poor quality supplies. Immigrant national communities formed their own battalions and often dressed in a style reminiscent of their homeland, such as French-styled tirialleurs or Zouaves or Italian Bersalergis.

The division into the Blue or the Grey gives a simplified view of the uniforms worn. It is true that this was the general difference in uniform colour, but the whole subject of military dress is beyond the scope of this book. The big factor involved was supply. If a regiment could obtain regulation issue clothing it did so, and was not too particular about what it received. There were units who took pride in their uniform appearance, some adopted a particular distinguishing feature such as the cocked black hat. Others wore civilian clothes and a variety of headgear. Some northern units wore grey and the odd southern unit wore blue, which led to mistakes and complaints. Confederate troops in the western theatres were more often in 'butternut' than grey, and some élite sharpshooters on both sides wore dark green in the European tradition. Regulation issue was usually the wool or thick cotton, shoddy, unshaped frock coat in dark blue or grey, straight jenner trousers of a faded blue and a soft cloth, peaked kepi. Facing colours, if present on collars, cuffs and kepis, were often 'arm-related', being light blue for the infantry, red for the artillery and yellow for the cavalry. However, there was the whole gamut of nineteenth-century military dress on display, including shell jackets, full frocks, sack coats, tunics and greatcoats, short shakoes, wide-brims, cutters and bowlers, breeches, overalls and baggy pants. The combinations were endless. As a rough rule, the degree of uniformity was better among the Northerners than the Confederates because they had the mass tailoring industry, although the South had the cotton. Officers tended to have their own tailors run up their own uniforms and only marginally adhered to regulations. Gold lacing was often quite liberal especially among the senior commanders, whose style of dress was frequently flamboyant and deliberately distinctive; a trait many were to regret, as good marksmen on both sides took a heavy toll among the 'gold-braids'.

However, no matter the style and colour of the uniform, the race, national origin or creed, each man ostensibly decided to fight himself, and to choose which side. Records tell us that in this 'civil' war not only were states and towns divided, but families too were split over the complex issues involved. When the 7th West Virginia was ordered forward to fight the Confederate

line at Gettysburg it found itself up against the 7th Virginia. This tragic irony was not lost on its Union commander, Lt-Col Lockwood, as among the officers they captured was his nephew. There is also a poignant story involving two infantrymen from Kentucky, who refused to shoot when they saw their father in the enemy line. Even at sea the fratricide went on. Capt Buchanan of the CSS *Virginia* sank the USS *Congress*, sending his brother to the bottom with her. Such tales abound in diaries, newspaper cuttings and records so that they rise above the level of folklore.

The speed with which men flocked to the Colours on both sides may indicate a depth of feeling that had been evolving for many years, but probably it had more to do with young men and rites of passage. The war proffered a coming of age with a just cause to follow. The cause of freedom was a popular, romantic myth that the whole country shared more than the notion of nationhood, and both sides raised its standard for its late teenagers and early twenty-year-olds. The War of Independence fuelled the romance of men fighting for their rights and liberties whereas the national army failed to prevent the British burning Washington in 1812. As well as being an outlet for the idealism of youth, the war was also an opportunity to settle grievances, especially with neighbours on a personal, town, city or state level. Petty and regional rivalries or revenge feuds were other motivating forces, and so too was opportunism. Wars bring chaos, and in disorder men can grab what they desire. It would be unfair to infer that such polyglot armies did not contain their share of opportunists and entrepreneurs both legal and criminal.

Discipline was a difficult concept for the 'land of the free'. Von Moltke said there was nothing military to learn from this war because it was fought by ill-disciplined, armed mobs herded about by incompetents or romantic fools. It was certainly different from the European tradition of warfare. The whole notion of a taut, impersonal discipline was alien to the vast influx of recruits. Early free and easy ways lessened but most armies never acquired the habit of unquestioning, immediate obedience nor the desire to snap to rigid attention as the Europeans deemed essential. As officers were often elected by the men or politically appointed by the State Governor, they needed to be liked by those they commanded – one day they would want their votes. These were not men to strike fear into or bear down upon their men, who would not respond positively if they did. West Point did its best in officer training but could not supply the number needed. Officers learnt on the job and even read tactical text books in their tents. Discipline in camp was never tight, on the march it never prevented straggling but in action it was often very good.

Training was basic; they did the rudimentary things like using the weapon, but most was concerned with getting into either marching or fighting formation. Strangely, there appears to be a lack of target practice in records and when it did happen it gave the lie to the idea that every American was a natural.

In a civil war, fathers, sons and brothers sometimes wore different uniform

The speed at which men flocked to the colours on both sides may indicate a depth of feeling that had been evolving for many years, but probably it had more to do with young men and rites of passages. The war proffered a coming of age with a just cause to follow

The cause of freedom was a popular, romantic myth that the whole country shared more than the notion of nationhood, and both sides raised their standard for their late teenagers and early twenty-year-olds

Rest and recreation were essential after frequent marches over long distances. These forced marches were mostly over open land, increasing the fatigue of the soldier

'Stonewall' Jackson marched his 160,000 men over 600 miles in thirty-five days during his Shenandoah Valley Campaign

During this time, they fought five battles

The following table edited from a Civil War Associate Research publication gives the statistics of war, but each figure is a 'rounded' approximation and each number was a man with an individual story:

	North	South
Regular Army 1861	16,400	0
In service between 1861 & '65	2,213,400	1,003,600
Strength July '61	219,400	114,000
Strength Jan '63	962,300	450,200
Strength '64/'65	1,044,660	484,800
Killed	110,100	94,000
Wounded	383,100	320,000
Missing	6,750	unknown
Captured	211,400	462,000
Died in prison	30,200	26,000
Died of disease	224,000	60,000
Other deaths	34,800	unknown
Desertions	199,000	83,400
Discharged	426,500	57,800
Surrendered 1865		174,223

There are 79 National Civil War cemeteries in which 54 per cent of the men buried are unidentified. The largest is at Vicksburg, where only 3,896 out of 16,000 are known. The fate of the unlucky common soldier was the common grave pit. At Salisbury prison 99 per cent of the 12,126 Union dead are unknown.

Life in the armed forces has changed little over the centuries, with boredom, hard labour and sheer terror being its three main constituents. However, during the American Civil War several factors varied this monotony a little. As strategic speed of movement was crucial to the operation of the war, the men spent long days and nights marching across the countryside in fast, forced marches rather than gradual advances. They often marched across the open land, leaving the roads, such as they were, to the wheeled vehicles. 'Stonewall' Jackson marched his 160,000 men over 600 miles in 35 days during his Shenandoah Valley Campaign. During this time they fought 5 battles and put 63,000 Union troops out of action. Long respites for rest and recreation were essential after such efforts, but as the men were volunteers the authorities had little intention of letting them depart from a theatre of war. The need to keep a standing army in the field and to keep it concentrated to resist lightning moves by the enemy meant the soldiers had to be housed together and consequently the men had long periods in army camps. Tents were issued in vast numbers and most men spent a long time in huge canvas cities. Set out like towns, the camp had its Army HQ at its heart, with streets running in straight lines towards its 'gates'. Based upon the Roman marching camps seen in the books at West Point and the Virginia Military Academy, the camp had a central parade ground and subsequent sections of the ground allocated to the various divisions and brigades. In turn, each brigade gave each regiment a space to erect its full complement of white duck ridge tents, which were home to up to ten men; transport lines, canteen and stores depot were also established. Most times there were Brigade and Regimental HQs, and drills and rotas for everything

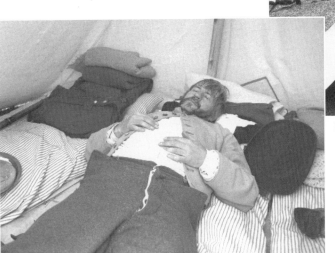

Most men spent long periods in huge tented camps

the military mind could conceive needed organising – even sports and team photographs. Civilian entry was usually permitted but, more often than not, a less well-ordered tent city sprawled outside the gates with saloons, brothels, shops and purveyors of every comfort a recruit's money could buy.

Often these camps were situated behind trench lines. Fieldworks were a major protection against artillery fire and even slit trenches for soldiers on picket duty were dug with alacrity. It has been estimated that Sherman's army, during its famous four-month march from Chattanooga to Atlanta, constructed over 300 miles of rifle pits. The Union forces also constructed 35 miles of trenches and fortifications during the campaign to take Petersburg. From these offensive works 175 field and siege guns bombarded the Confederate defensive lines with nearly 8 tons of iron every day. The heavier the bombardment the deeper they dug and the more protection they got. It is significant that in this first modern war the men dug in under fire, they constructed fieldworks and lines of both offensive and defensive trench systems. These trenches were either literally holes in the earth or quite complicated, engineered complexes of sandbags, gabions, log revetments and duckboards, with underground magazines and blockhouse gun positions. If the European military had bothered to study America in the 1860s they would have seen that two reasonably equally equipped modern armies in the face of such weaponry dig themselves into the earth to avoid being mown down.

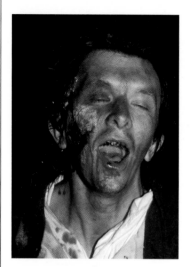

The wounded of the American Civil War were more likely to survive than their European counterparts. Both North and South had medical facilities, although standards varied greatly. But the real menace was disease – twice as many men died from this killer than as a direct result of the fighting

In the trenches and in the field, rations were a constant worry to both armies. On campaign, soldiers rarely had the amounts the commissariat were supposed to supply. On paper, Union troops in 1864 had 1¼ lb of meat and 1¼ lb of flour per day, along with dry beans, green coffee and sugar. In reality it was far less. Things were worse in the Confederate lines; there, every 100 men had to share 4 lb of bacon, 1½ lb of flour, 10 lb of rice and a small quantity of dried peas and dried fruit. This effectively meant thay had to subsist off the land. The commissariat of both sides had a very hard time acquiring the necessary amounts of provisions and when they did scrape together loads they had an even harder time distributing it to the men in the field. The South tried over-land distribution taking supplies to the firing line, while the North used centralised depots and collection points. This was made simpler for the Union because of its control of a good railway network. The greatest military use for trains was in the transport of supplies, both raw materials and war products, and for the rapid strategic deployment of reinforcements; but they were targets for raids and sabotage. They brought the material of war to the fighting and carried its detritus back again. There were even special hospital trains to ferry the wounded from the battle area to hospitals in the north, although problems for the injured men were far from over when they arrived at overcrowded and underresourced institutions.

Still, the wounded had a better chance of survival than many of those hit on a European battlefield, and both North and South had field and back-up military hospitals. The quality of the hospitals varied enormously, as did the expertise of the surgeons and doctors. Some were excellent, while others were appalling. The only thing they had in common was the large number of men who came through their blood-soaked hands. Union hospital records show that they dealt with over 6,000,000 men during the war, although the death ratio was 2:1 disease to bullets. Outbreaks of diarrhoea and dysentery were common and at times reached epidemic proportions – 44,558 Union soldiers are known to have died from these two killers alone.

A soldier's life was not an easy one and the new long-range, fast-firing weapons made it a more dangerous one than people pre-war could have imagined. Although possibly not frequently discussed, many had a basic belief in the cause for which they fought and diaries show a general tendency to sentimentalism and self-pity. Photographs and etchings depict campfire camaraderie, and intense loyalty from a man to his friends and his unit was common. Overall, the men of this first modern war were like soldiers throughout time: tough, resilient, often sardonic and mostly ready to take whatever fate had in store.

THEIR WEAPONS

Rifles: The most common weapon of the war was the rifle. However, there were over 100 different regulation-issue models of rifle and carbine in use, not to mention the diverse collection of unofficial patterns. Most rifles could

Like soldiers throughout time: tough, resilient, often sardonic and mostly ready to take whatever fate had in store

send a bullet over 800 yd – sometimes over 1,000 yd, but effective range was often much less. Most were long-barrelled and muzzle-loading, and were fired by percussion cap. The lengthy loading process associated with the Brown Bess or the Chassepot was still necessary until the radical introduction of the breech-loader, which gave its users a much greater rate of fire and a distinct battlefield advantage – not to mention improved morale. Technological advance saw the introduction of the repeating rifle with a magazine of cartridges and an action that ejected the spent case. These again revolutionised rates of fire but production and heat expansion problems

The most common weapon of the war was the rifle. However, there were over 100 different regulation-issue models of rifle and carbine in use, not to mention the diverse collection of unofficial patterns. Most rifles could send a bullet over 800 yd – sometimes up to 1,000 yd, but effective range was much less. Most were long-barrelled and muzzle-loading, and were fired by percussion cap

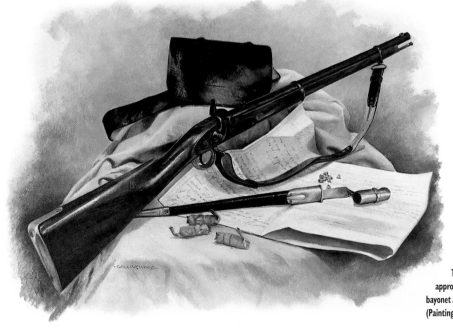

Tower Percussion 2 band musket, 1865, approximately .577 cal, with the Enfield short bayonet and scabbard and Enfield cartridge box. (Painting by Chris Collingwood; see Useful Addresses)

meant they were more likely to jam than the older models. To go into the detail of each of these weapons is beyond the scope of this book, but the chart below should help the enthusiast to pursue the interest more fully:

Model	Calibre (in)	Range (yd)	Shots (per min)	Misfires	Nos used
US Musket 1822 model, Flintlock	.69	70	2–3	1/6	
US Rifle 1841 model	.54/.58	200	1–2		100,000
US Percussion Musket 1842 model	.69	100	2–3	1/166	150,000
US Rifled Musket 1855 model Maynard primer	.58	500	1–2		47,000
US Rifled Springfield Percussion Musket 1861/63	.58	300	3–6		1,700,000
Enfield Rifle Musket	.577	500	2–3		800,000
Remington Rifle Musket 1863 model	.58	500	1–2		39,000
Whitworth Rifle	.451	800	1		100
Sharps Breech-loading Rifle	.52	600	6–9		11,000
Spencer Breech-loading Rifle	.52	500	9–20		62,000
Henry Rifle	.44	450	30–50		10,000

The most popular rifle was the US Rifle Musket model 1861, known as the 'Springfield Rifle' because of its initial manufacture at the Springfield Armoury in Massachusetts. Later in the war other factories were set up under licence to turn out these efficient weapons. They were used on both sides and the Confederacy made a considerable haul when they captured 150,000 of them. The 1861 pattern was produced with two modifications, 1863.1 and 1863.2. The original weapon used the Maynard firing system but this was quickly replaced by the usual percussion cap. Like most rifles it had a much longer range than the smooth-bore musket, the Springfield being capable of hitting at 1,000 yd, although for effective fire 300 yd was considered the optimum distance. Its one drawback was that it was muzzle-loading and consequently much slower than the breech-loading rifles that followed it. It also had to be reloaded standing up and, in going through the longer drill required to load the soldier presented a reasonable and stationary target to his opposite number.

It took eleven separate actions to load and fire an American Civil War rifle and the 1860 regulations state that a soldier should allow 2 seconds per action and get one shot off every 20 seconds enabling a rate of fire of three rounds per minute – arithmetic does not seem to have been a strong feature of military planning.

By far the best breech-loading rifle was the Spencer, which also had a repeater mechanism and fired an 8-shot preloaded magazine. An experienced soldier could fire up to twenty-one rounds per minute, which could mean a battalion effectively wiping out an enemy unit armed with something slower. One thing in the Union's favour with the Spencer was its use of the copper cartridge. The Confederacy had no means to manufacture this ammunition, thus a captured Spencer, although excellent in the short term because of its rate of fire, was useless when the cartridges ran out. The fastest repeater was the Henry with its 15-shot magazine that could be emptied in just 11 seconds. Including magazine changing time, it could fire

120 rounds in 6 minutes. A Union campaign-strength regiment of 500 men armed with Henry rifles could lay down a devastating field of fire of 20,000 rounds in 1 minute as opposed to a similarly sized Confederate unit firing 1,500 rounds with the US 1842 Percussion Musket. In addition, men using a breech-loader could reload kneeling or even prone, thus presenting a much reduced or even negligible target. At Stone's River the Union Army shot over 2,000,000 bullets in three days, while effectiveness can be judged by a calculation that estimated an average of 9,000 bullets were fired for each man killed or wounded at First Bull Run.

It is interesting to note that even armed with the more sophisticated weapons, it is the men and their ability to drill that decides the day. Recruits or raw volunteers, who have terror to distract them, inexperienced troops or even regulars unused to being shot at or operating among the din and carnage of war, even veterans in the frenzy of action, can frequently forget vital sections of reloading drill. Firing away the ramrod, putting the bullet down before the charge, reversing the nose of the bullet or even loading on top of misfires were common errors that could render even a precision repeating rifle no more useful than a club. Study of the records concerning weapons picked up at Gettysburg revealed that of 37,000 muskets gathered together, 24,000 were loaded, 18,000 of which had more than one charge down the barrel. One terrified soldier had rammed twenty-three rounds on top of a chargeless bullet. American battlefield statisticians have deduced from these and other figures that 35 per cent of the men at Gettysburg were ineffective because of the misuse of their weapons.

Carbines: Like its Napoleonic predecessor, the carbine was the longarm for cavalry. It was not a scaled-down version of a manufacturer's rifle, but a particularly designed weapon for use on horseback as well as in dismounted tactics. The carbine had a much shorter barrel and a smaller calibre, making it lighter, easier to balance and feasible to fire one-handed. At the

Carbine used by cavalry. Its shorter length made it more convenient to use in the saddle

beginning of the war, the carbine too was a muzzle-loader, which rendered it a single-shot weapon in mounted action. Considerable numbers of the British Enfield carbine were imported and issued to both sides during 1861–2, but the armouries of the North soon developed a breech-load action for their products. While the Union adopted the Spencer and the Sharps carbine in vast numbers, the muzzle-loader remained popular with the Confederacy. Again the models vary and another chart should help readers understand their differences:

Model	Calibre (in)	Range (yd)	Shots (per min)	Nos used
Spencer Breech-loading Carbine	.52	400	9–20	94,000
Sharps Breech-loading Carbine	.52	400	9–15	80,000
Burnside Carbine	.54	200	3–5	55,000
Smith Carbine	.52	200		30,000
Maynard Breech-loading Percussion Carbine	.5	150		20,000
Starr Breech-loading Percussion Carbine	.54	200		25,000
Gallager Breech-loading Percussion Carbine	.54	150		22,000
Joslyn Breech-loading Carbine	.52	150		10,000
Enfield Muzzle-loading Carbine	.577	200	2–3	40,000

The Spencer was the best carbine of the war and its rapid rate of fire made it a combat-winning weapon. It did have a problem with degrees of accuracy, which was exacerbated by the men firing off as fast as the weapon would permit and taking little time or care to aim. However, it certainly influenced Union and later US cavalry tactics, making them more firepower oriented. The southern mounted arm's preference for the slower but more accurate Enfield or the 'Richmond Sharps' influenced their tactical thinking. Confederate cavalrymen also had a predilection for double-barrelled shotguns.

Pistols: The American Constitution grants every citizen the right to bear arms and apparently many volunteers turned up at recruiting depots carrying their own pistols, some purchased specially for the war. The pistol was the favourite weapon of the Confederate cavalry, particularly among the early-raised units for whom it was often the only weapon. Pistols of all designs, makes and age were brought out for use, including many outdated flintlocks. Patterns varied considerably and some designs even had detachable shoulderstocks to help with aiming and recoil. It must have been a nightmare for ammunition supply officers. The Union government bought 374,000 revolvers alone, the Confederacy set up factories to copy the more successful northern manufacturers' ware, while importers from both sides ordered substantial numbers from Europe. Of the huge numbers of pistols used, the ones below were the more popular weapons:

Model	Calibre (in)	Nos used
Colt Revolver 1848 Dragoon Pattern	.44	90,000
Colt Revolver 1851 Navy Pattern	.36	200,000
Colt Revolver 1860 Army Pattern	.44	320,000
Remington New Model Revolver	.44	125,000
Remington Navy Revolver	.36	
Starr Revolver Army Pattern	.44 (.36 Navy)	48,000
US Springfield Single Shot	.58	
Savage Navy Revolver	.36	11,000
Whitney Revolver	.36	11,000
Lefaucheaux Revolver	.41	12,000
Deane & Adams Five Shot Revolver	.44	
Le Mat Revolver	.40	3,000

At the beginning of the war, the single-shot pistol was in common use, such as the Palmetto Percussion pistol of South Carolina or the US Springfield. Gradually, various revolving mechanisms were designed, most around a series of chambers in a rotating cylinder block, and produced in great numbers. This increased the rate of fire considerably. Then the self-cocking double-action radically increased it again; hitherto the hammer had to be pulled back by hand, like cocking a flintlock. Coupled with the

Walker Colt .44 cal 4 lb 9 oz Holster Pistol 1847, with Walker flask, c. 1860, cavalry sabre and military cloth-covered canteen. (Painting by Chris Collingwood; see Useful Addresses)

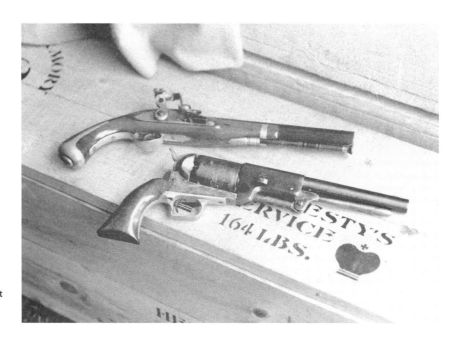

Pistols of all designs, makes and ages were brought out for use, including many outdated flintlocks (top)

introduction of the self-consuming cartridge replacing the individual-chamber powder and ball reload, the rapidity of shots increased dramatically. So quickly could a six-shooter be emptied that many men, especially troopers, took to carrying several pistols – six appears to be the maximum. Each manufacturer vied with competitors to grab the lucrative pistol trade, many southern gunsmiths, such as Griswolf & Gunnison and the Dance Brothers, bought examples of the best in the North and copied them, even improving on their efficiency and adding their own innovations.

Bayonets: Almost every infantryman on both sides was issued with a bayonet but they were very infrequently used in combat. Muzzle-loading with a fixed bayonet can be hazardous, especially if the blade has been honed to razor sharpness, and making one's way through woodland or scrub can be hindered by the 18-in extension. They were constructed of reasonable quality steel and not so prone to buckling as early nineteenth-century models. Most were socket type and fitted over the barrel, and were held by a welded lug. Sword bayonets were popular with Zouave units and their kin, but these were more a part of the showy uniform rather than a fighting weapon.

Machine-guns: Both sides tried volley guns and machine-guns to increase the rate of fire along their lines. Again there were several different types with different qualities:

Model	No. of barrels	Calibre (in)	Loading	Range (yd)	Shots (per min)
Williams Gun	1	1.57	Paper cartridge	2,000	18–20
Agar Gun	1	.58	Paper cartridge	1,000	120
Gatling Gun 1862 model	6	.58	Brass case	2,000	250
Billinghurst Reque	25	.25	Paper cartridge	1,200	175
Vandenberg Volley gun	85–450	.58		500	85–450

The Williams was first used in action at Seven Pines in May 1862. It was a breech-loader mounted upon a small carriage usually reserved for a mountain howitzer. However, the breech often expanded with the heat of the firing and consequently jammed. The Agar was a favourite of Lincoln's and he pushed the Union Army into accepting it. It had a light carriage and a steel shield to protect the gunners. At Middlesburg, two Agars of the 28th Pennsylvania Volunteers virtually destroyed two Confederate cavalry troops at 800 yd but despite this effective performance it was phased out of field use. The famous Gatling was also prone to jamming and the improved 1865 model, which resolved many of its problems and increased its rate of fire and its range, came into production too late for use in the war.

The Artillery: There are records of at least 266 different types of pieces of artillery being used during the Civil War, so once again a chart shows the attributes of the varied yet more common guns used. Types were suited to specific projectiles, smooth-bores using spherical, while rifles fired cylindro-conoidal ammunition, but each type had its good points and its bad, its supporters and its detractors:

Model	Barrel	Calibre (in)	Weight (lb)	Round (lb)	Charge (lb)	Range (yd)
12-pdr Napoleon 1857	Smooth	4.62	1,227	12.3	2.5	1,680
6-pdr 1841	Smooth	3.67	884	6.1	1.25	1,520
12-pdr 1841–4	Smooth	4.62	1,757	12.3	2.5	1,660
12-pdr howitzer 1841	Smooth	4.62	788	8.9	0.75	1,072
24-pdr 1841–4	Smooth	5.82	1,318	18.0	2.0	1,322
32-pdr howitzer 1841–4	Smooth	6.2	1,920	25.0	2.5	1,500
12-pdr mountain howitzer	Smooth	2.0	220	8.9	0.75	900
10-pdr Parrott 1861	Rifled	3.0	890	9.5	1.0	2,970
20-pdr Parrott 1861	Rifled	3.67	1,750	20.0	2.0	4,400
3-in Rodman 1863	Rifled	3.0	820	9.5	1.0	2,788
6-pdr Wiard	Rifled	2.65	425			800
12-pdr Wiard	Rifled	3.6	785		0.3	1,850
6-pdr Whitworth	Rifled	2.15	700		0.75	2,750
12-pdr Whitworth BL	Rifled	2.75	1,100	12.0	1.75	8,800
12-pdr Whitworth ML	Rifled	2.75	1,090	12.0	1.75	3,000
12-pdr Armstrong	Rifled	3.0	918	12.0	1.75	2,100
12-pdr Armstrong ML	Rifled	3.0	1,009	12.0	1.75	2,200
Mounted Rifle	Rifled	2.25		3.0		1,100
Brooke Gun	Rifled	3.0		10.0		3,500

There were other manufacturers of small quantities of artillery, including English imports like the Blakely, with variations in calibre and poundage. The 12-pdr Napoleon was reliable and commonly used by both sides, but not the most predominant, as usually written. The old smooth-bore guns gradually gave way to the rifled ones, which had the longer ranges. McClellan in the Seven Days' Battles had 45 per cent Napoleons and the Confederates none at all. In some cases, such as the 6-pdr Whitworth, rifling and precision casting resulted in restricting fire to solid shot, the long, thin shell not having sufficient space to accommodate a powerful exploding charge. Overall, the British imports seem to have produced astonishing accuracy and served the Confederacy especially well, but their cost was often prohibitive. The weight of an artillery piece was also an important consideration. The lighter it was the more manoeuvrable and quicker to deploy; it was also more easily evacuated when under threat. The 12-pdr 1841–4 smooth-bore was as effective as the Napoleon and could outreach its effective range but it was 530 lb heavier, which made it less popular and more difficult to transport on campaign. The lightest piece was the 12-pdr mountain howitzer, which could be broken down and carried on pack mules. This was exceptionally useful for infantry support in difficult terrain, such as mountainous country, and for keeping up with skirmishers, and an experienced crew could assemble and fire off one round in less than 1 minute. Naturally, people had preferences for particular models. The 3-in Rodman, developed by the US Ordnance Department, was lightweight but had a considerable range making it a favourite of the Horse Artillery. To simplify supply, the Ordnance Department insisted that many Union 10-pdr Parrotts were modified to take the same ammunition as the Rodman. Some guns were not in favour. Lee

Confederate artillery

strongly criticised the performance of the 6-pdr 1841–4, going so far as to urge that all 6-pdrs be melted down to produce 12s.

There were four main types of ammunition: *solid shot*, which passed through ranks of soldiers, bouncing several times if round, and carving swathes through dense formations; *shell*, which was hollow-cast and full of explosive, with a time or impact fuse. Upon explosion, shells fragmented into about seven pieces, all of which would tear lanes through units. Heavier shells were called *bombs* and were reserved for the mortars; *shrapnel*, which was again a hollow-cast projectile but full of explosive and musket balls – seventy-eight in a shrapnel shell for a 12-pdr Napoleon. It usually had a cut timed fuse that burst the shell directly overhead of its target, spraying the balls and the chunks of casing in all directions. The final common projectile was *canister*, a tin tube filled with golf-ball sized balls – twenty-seven in a canister case for a 12-pdr Napoleon. The tin casing tore apart in the firing and the gun spewed out the balls in a deadly funnel over a range of 400 yd before running out of momentum. Post-Gettysburg, light canister was introduced, with even smaller, marble or grape-sized balls packed in a tin can; it had a devastating effect at point-blank range but had neither the stopping power nor the range of the heavier variety. Most guns fired shot and shell but canister sometimes had a detrimental effect on the grooving of certain manufacturers' rifled barrels.

As well as field pieces there was another considerable range of siege, naval and garrison artillery. These were the big guns used to batter defences, pound advancing columns or smash ships. They ranged from the 4.63 cal. 12-pdr to the 10.0 cal. 330-pdr Parrott and the massive 20-in Rodman that could hurl its 1,080-lb projectile some 3½ miles. Most popular in sieges were the big-bellied, stubby mortars that could lob shells behind walls or into trenches. They were difficult to transport because of their weight and some were mounted on railway flat trucks and trained to their firing point, often using the rails to guide and distribute the recoil from their powerful blast. The various popular types are recorded below:

Model	Weight of Shell (lb)	Range (yd)
8-in	44.5	1,200
10-in	87.5	2,100
24-pdr Coehorn 5.82 inch	17	1,200
10-in garrison	87.5	4,250
13-in	220	4,325

Many guns had 'names', being 'christened' by the gunners who worked them rather than cast into the barrel in the French Napoleonic style. The most famous was probably the railway-mounted mortar called 'Dictator', which was used by the Union at Petersburg. The Navies too had a range of guns and some 'came ashore' mounted on field carriages for field use, the most usual being the 12-pdr howitzer 4.6 with a range of 1,085 yd, which was often used by the Union Navy for amphibious landing operations.

Stuart is known to have used Congreve rockets, which had not attracted investment since 1815 and consequently were about as useful as they ever were. The Union had Hale rockets of 6- and 16-pdr varieties. They had a supposed range of 2,200 yd but once again accuracy was rare and performance erratic. Effective rockets were too much of a technological development for this first modern war.

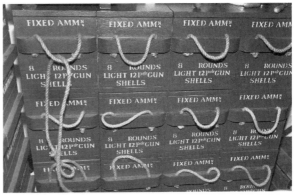

Swords were carried principally by officers, as badges of rank

Sabres: The North manufactured a variety of sabres based upon the curve-bladed US Army issue pattern. The Confederacy had no real sabre production line and relied instead upon imported stocks from Europe. Both Britain and France supplied quantities of old-fashioned or second-rate goods, including the ubiquitous English 1796 pattern light cavalry cutting weapon. Prussia exported a number of straight-bladed heavy cavalry sabres from the Soligen works.

Some swords were also carried, principally by officers, as badges of rank. They were officially issued to all infantry officers, senior NCOs, musicians and artillerymen and were usually straight-bladed and quite delicate for the work they were supposed to do. Issues were not frequent and a pistol was the preferred weapon. The short artillery sword was a particularly useless implement, even its best use – chopping wood – being bettered by an ordinary axe.

Other personal weapons: Photographs of the period show many men displaying an assortment of big, heavy knives. Popular with the volunteers of the more western armies, many were somewhat strange copies of the

'Bowie' pattern knife. Too big to be a good camp knife and of very little use in action, they were often discarded. The pike too was another useless weapon that made an appearance. The Confederate government wasted money and production by insisting that every southern regiment should have two companies of pikemen and turned out vast numbers of stocks to equip them. They were never issued and the men for whom they were intended could only be grateful. Some were given to civilians to stem the Union advance in the later stages of the war but the 'town armies' never mustered when threatened.

Very popular in Europe during the 1860s, the lance was almost ignored in favour of firearms. The Americans realised the lance had finally had its day in combat against modern armies. There were several lancer, or so-called, units, indeed the 6th Pennsylvanian Cavalry are known to have purchased a supply and carried them for a while. The US government also bought over 90,000 Ketcham grenades, whose crude delayed-ignition system worked reasonably well, but the manufacturers, Excelsior, could not get the timing right and their grenades had a tendency to explode in the hand before being thrown and were consequently unpopular. Some old-fashioned 6-pdr shells with attached fuses were hand lit and rolled down steep glacis (banks sloping down from a fort, on which attackers are exposed to defenders' missiles) – another hit and miss affair.

THEIR FIGHTING

Army organisation was based upon European models with the core unit being the regiment. Most regular regiments had 2 to 4 battalions and although they often served apart, instances can be found of them serving in pairs. Each regular battalion was composed of 8 companies but 10 was popular for volunteers. There were also independent battalions of anything from 3 to 6 companies. Company strength on paper was 100 men, being 3 officers, 13 NCOs, 2 musicians and 82 privates. Each company was further divided into 2 platoons, each with 4 sections and 8 squads. A regiment also had a HQ staff of 3 field officers and a senior NCO, with an officer and 2 NCOs for each of the administration, medical and stores services. Field strength varied according to campaign and replacements. The following chart gives approximate battalion strengths in the field:

Year	North	South	
1861	700	600	From these figures the Union policy of sending replacement regiments in the field is evident.
1862	500	450	
1863	320	350	The Confederacy fought a losing struggle to keep their fast-diminishing units up to strength.
1864	400	250	
1865	500	150	

Confederate First Lieutenant

The cavalry were formed into regiments with the basic movement unit being the squadron. Both sides started the war with 5 squadrons composed of 2 companies each, which was further divided into 2 platoons of 30 to 40 troopers. In July 1861 the Union changed its tactical thinking and its organisation, creating regiments of 3 battalions of 2 squadrons, thus 12 companies or 24 platoons of 20 to 30 troopers. Field strengths were considerably different and as the Union battalions sustained losses, so the new battalions reverted to the role of squadrons. Regimental strengths averaged: early years – North, 360; South, 280; later years – North, 250; South, 200.

Horse breeding was a tradition in the South and horse ownership a thing of pride and universal interest. For the early part of the war, many Confederate squadrons were mounted on bloodstock and their casts, so men who had spent their lives in the saddle as ranch hands, cowboys and farm boys and who owned their horses and bred them as a matter of course could literally run rings around those who rode only when necessary or even had to be taught to ride and who were mounted on government-purchased, cheap, and usually quite sorry nags. Should a southern cavalryman have his own horse killed in action, initially he got compensation and leave to return home to get another. As the years went by, payments dried up and replacement mounts were hard to find. The North had 'used up' the cheap sources and had the cash to buy the remaining better stock. The balance in quality of mount gradually shifted but it was not until 1863 that they met on vaguely equal terms.

The artillery were divided into heavy and light regiments. The heavy artillery were raised for the big guns, 20-pdrs and heavier, and mostly fought in siege or fortified defensive actions. They were organised into 12 companies, formed in to 3 battalions of 400 men in each. The light artillery were raised for battlefield field duty and divided into foot and horse organisations, both using combinations of the lighter guns; mostly 12- or 6-pdrs. The major difference was that horse gunners rode their own mounts alongside their guns and could consequently move faster and support daring cavalry raids or campaigns, while field or foot gunners marched or rode on the carriage or caissons and were principally infantry support. The artillery who manned the guns were divided into regiments of

Below, left: Confederate NCOs – First Sergeant (left), Sergeant (right); centre: Confederate privates; right: Union officer (left), Union private (right)

3 batteries in the Union and 4 in the Confederacy, with the battery being the principal unit of tactical deployment. In the early stages, Union batteries, commanded by a captain, had 6 guns to the Confederate's 4; later the Union reduced to 4. Thus, for the majority of the war, each battery comprised 2 sections of 2 guns; with each gun, 9 crew, 6 drivers, 1 limber with 6 horses, and 1 caisson with 6 horses, forming a platoon under an NCO. Sections were capable of operating separately under a lieutenant. The South mixed types – 1 section of smooth-bores and the other rifled pieces – while the North tended to have all one type to a battery. Each battery comprised, on paper, 155 men, including officers, NCOs, gunners, drivers, musicians and blacksmiths – it also had a travelling forge and work wagon. Field strengths were less. At Gettysburg, Union batteries were down to 105 men while Confederate batteries were at 90. Teams too were reduced to 4. To stay in action effectively, a gun needed a minimum of 3 crew despite the heroic deeds of certain individuals.

The North was superior in its artillery arm to the South, mainly because of its industrial background and financial resources. The North could afford to make more guns and had the factories to do it. The number of Union guns usually outnumbered those of the Confederacy on any battlefield and, more often than not, the North had a higher percentage of the modern rifled pieces. There was also a perception that the northern recruits, being more 'process-oriented' and more used to servicing machinery, had a greater aptitude for the artillery than the southern ranch and farm workers.

Most higher organisation was as separate 'arms' although, in the early years and in the western theatre, mixed arm brigades sometimes featured. However, usually between 2 and 6 infantry regiments made a brigade; 3 Union or 4 Confederate brigades formed a division; and 2 divisions formed

Confederate General

Below, left: Union 1st Lieutenant; right: Union Cavalry Trooper

a corps. Confederate brigades were often formed of regiments from the same state, something which the Union did with the Philadelphia Brigade.

The range of the rifle and the availability of newer patterns were key factors in battlefield tactics. Early in the war both sides, being relatively equally equipped, marched onto the field in open column of companies formed in lines four deep – the distance between each company was calculated to allow each company to wheel into a battalion line. Each regiment formed to attack with six companies in line with two in reserve about 150 yd back and two companies about 300 yd in front, skirmishing with a small skirmish reserve 50 yd behind them. They advanced upon each other, with the skirmishers falling back to the reserve or to the flanks as they were engulfed. When they stood about 100 yd apart they began a firefight, gradually closing the range, the side inflicting the most casualties being more anxious to get closer to do greater damage. The reserve was committed as the line thinned or shortened. The nerve of one side would eventually give, and the loser would fall back in whatever state its morale permitted. Sometimes a weakened regiment would be replaced in the battleline by a fresh one that would restore the balance through its greater numbers.

As the technological war stepped up, breech-loaders made it possible to fire faster so the casualties came quicker and the advances speeded up – nobody liked to spend a long time under fire without firing back. Several regiments trained to advance in the French chasseur manner – very quickly in loose order only to halt at close range and fire. Some Zouave units adopted chasseur tactics and actually committed themselves to using their sword bayonets by attacking unloaded. However, better rifling and better ammunition production meant ranges increased so, in general, the fire-fights started further apart. It is a strange fact, nonetheless, that although in defensive positions infantrymen would open fire at 500 to 600 yd (when attacking or meeting in open fields), 150 yd was considered the maximum, even with the newer rifles. At Vicksburg, Union troops attacked over 700 yd of cleared terrain only to stop, dig in and fire from the earth at the Confederate fortifications, at a range of 10 to 20 yd. To deal with fire received while attacking prepared infantry, some units became sharp shooters, working their way forward in open order and using available cover, lying prone to fire and allowing the next line to go forward and establish itself before they continued this leapfrog advance.

The main problem for officers came when the enemy had superior weapons. As late as 1862 many Confederates carried the old-fashioned flintlock, US 1822 model, smooth-bore musket; it was a muzzle-loader with a maximum effective range of 100 yd, with a 1 in 6 misfire rate that was even worse in wet weather. Up against the US 1855 model, rifled musket, reasonably accurate up to 500 yd, with a 1 in 25 misfire rate (even before the Maynard tape priming system was replaced), the southern infantry encountered a severe disadvantage – they could match or even beat

Each regiment formed to attack with six companies in line, with two in reserve about 150 yd back

Two companies were approximately 300 yd in front, skirmishing with a small skirmish reserve 50 yd behind them

They advanced upon each other, with the skirmishers falling back to the reserve or to the flanks as they were engulfed

When they stood about 100 yd apart they began a firefight . . .

. . . gradually closing the range . . .

. . . the side inflicting the most casualties being more anxious to get closer to do greater damage

The nerve of one side would eventually give, and the loser would fall back in whatever state its morale permitted . . .

... leaving to the victor the spoils of war

the rate of fire but they were 400 yd short in range and had a huge number of misfires. The only tactic available in open ground was to advance rapidly to close range and deliver a shattering point-blank volley, hoping the speed of advance would reduce their own casualty rate and their own fire would shatter the morale of the Union men. It was a brave and optimistic officer who led such an advance. However, the training and expertise of the men was a major factor when firing beyond close range. It is believed that apart from the western troops fighting for the Union, the country-raised Confederates were usually more than a match for the factory-fodder of the North and would have an advantage in any 'fair' firefight. But even taking that into consideration, the work of Livermore suggests that, overall, the hit probability was low at long range (about 300–600 yd), but at close range the damage could be terrible. For comparison, in 5 minutes of firing on the second day of Gettysburg, Barksdale's 1,600 Confederates killed 570 out of 1,516 of Graham's Federals at just over 200 yd; but on the first day, in one exchange of volleys at a range of 20 yd, the 24th Michigan lost 397 out of 496 men and the 26th North Carolina lost 549 out of 800 men.

Better rifles with repeating actions made the contest even more uneven. For men to discover on the battlefield that the enemy could lay down fields of withering fire to which they could only sporadically reply, was enough to cause a retreat. An entrenched Kantian notion of fairness in the men can present field and general officers with interesting situations. One answer was entrenchment, and another was the bayonet charge. Bayonet charges are favourite topics of painters, writers and film-makers but although many valiant charges took place in the Civil War, surprisingly few came to 'the steel'. The small number that did result in hand-to-hand fighting, such as the 17th Wisconsin's charge at Corinth, were recorded for their rarity. Union wound returns give a convincing picture: of 7,302 in the Wilderness Campaign only 6 had bayonet wounds; and of 250,000 in hospital in the whole war only 922 had bayonet or sword wounds and many of these were the outcome of camp fights. More often than not, 'charges' came to a stop with both sides blazing away at very close range until one side fled. This was exceptionally costly, especially when one side had the advantage of cover such as a wall or a split rail fence. At Gettysburg the 26th North Carolina lost 708 out of 800 over the three days.

To encourage the men to go in with the bayonet, they sometimes deployed in column; this formation also had the effect of concentrating troops at a tactical point of weakness, thus forcing the issue. Companies were still in lines four deep, but arranged at intervals of 10 yd, one behind the other for 'closed column of companies', or two companies wide for 'closed column of divisions'. Closed columns were easier for the officers to control than open columns or lines but they presented easy targets. The theory was that the high casualties sustained in a short burst of a charge

Some infantry units became sharpshooters, lying prone to fire and allowing the next line to move forward and establish itself before they continued this leapfrog advance

would be less than those incurred in a firefight and it would often be decisive. Sometimes the ability to pick off the officers made a difference. An American tactic from the War of Independence, shooting officers was practised by both sides as a means of breaking 'charges' – bereft of its leaders, orders, example and encouragement, a column could falter and fall back.

Entrenchment was a back-breaking and soul-destroying occupation although, when completed, the trenches afforded substantial protection from shot and shell. Mostly earth and timber constructions, the whole range of field fortifications from English Civil War designs, through Vauban to the latest network of covered communication trenches and tunnels were employed. Assaulting these works was a deadly game. In an attack upon the Petersburg works, the 1st Maine Artillery Regiment lost 604 men in about 15 minutes.

Higher levels of command deployed different tactical formations. They too were influenced by the study of Napoleon's campaigns and battles. Flexibility was the keynote. Brigades usually drew up in successive lines as open column of regiments in action, or closed column of regiments in reserve. Divisions sometimes combined the two orders, with two brigades in line of regiments, one behind the other, and a third in column of regiments in reserve. Newton used the French *division ordre mixte* at Fredricksburg with his central brigade having three regiments in line abreast, with the fourth skirmishing for the whole division, and his two flank brigades in regimental columns of division. Despite the notion of fighting in lines, American Civil War troops were often deployed in dense masses, especially when undergoing tactical reposition or across rivers or between obstacles. The variation, effectiveness and stories of American Civil War grand-scale tactics lies outside the scope of this book, but it is interesting to note that as the company lines thinned from 4 through 3 to 2 in an effort to cover the allocated ground, so the density of the formations increased. Jackson went in at Chancellorsville with 150 yd between divisions deployed in line of brigades with their regiments in column, but at Shiloh the Confederates attacked in waves of corps. Not only did this lead to high casualties but also to chaos, as units became intermingled and confused. The tactic of advancing until stopped, then lying down to fire and allowing the next attack to pass over was often a further aid to confusion. Zook's brigade passed over Barnes' Division at Gettysburg while the 1st Maine Heavy Artillery, full of enthusiasm and martial spirit, did it to their cost at Petersberg. Both the massed attack in so-called lines and the passing over of bogged down units were features of the American Civil War and presaged the débâcles of the First World War.

Cavalry tactics for both sides derived from the French 'Poinsett Tactics' of 1841, which advocated companies formed columns of four to march, and the two-deep line to engage. On the battlefield they would adopt close column of squadrons if shock action was intended, and open column of

At full gallop, the cavalry could cover 400 yd per minute but frequently lost order

squadrons for the more usual attack. They seldom went into a full regimental line of squadrons as it would have been difficult to control. Each squadron took about 60 yd of frontage and walk-marched 150 yd per minute; at fast canter they got up to 300 yd and at full gallop they could cover 400 yd but frequently lost order.

However, the weapons carried by the cavalry determined the tactics they adopted as much as their drill manuals and fighting spirit. The North purchased and issued Spencer and Sharps carbines, which were reasonably accurate at 450 yd, while the South stayed with the old-fashioned muzzle-loading Enfield. Union horse consequently preferred long-range engagements, often dismounting, going into open order and seeking cover – typical dragoon tactics. For dismounted action one man in four was delegated to loop reins and hold the horses, taking them to the rear. The dismounted regiment formed line of eight companies in skirmish order, with two companies in advance in extended order, but with another

Above and opposite: Union cavalry often dismounted, going into open order and seeking cover – typical dragoon tactics

company, still mounted, deployed on each flank to provide support or cover. The Confederates, however, tended to remain mounted, discharging their carbines at 200 yd and then charging into closer action to blaze away with shotguns and then pistols, resorting to the sabre only when the ammunition was spent. Contrary to movie history, the dramatic sabre charge into the cut and slash of mêlée was not a typical style engagement. Both sides relied more on their guns than on the outdated sabre, although it did occupy the minds of several officers whose romantic notions paid off occasionally but more frequently they led their men to expensive failure.

These sabre charges were reinforced unintentionally by the thinking behind the 1861 reorganisation of the cavalry regiment into battalions, one to attack, one to support and one to countercharge if necessary. To be in third battalion meant official endorsement to take the opportunity of a romantic cavalry charge and, on occasions, presumed threats gave *carte blanche* for such a hedonistic and militarily unsound action. To charge hell for leather with an outstretched arm bearing a sabre is no mean feat, but a cavalry charge usually required reasonably open ground where the ranks of troopers would be exposed to galling fire. The ranges possible with massed rifles, and the rapid rates of fire with the newer patterns, meant charges were easily broken up if the infantry had the nerve to stand. One general's memoirs recall the folly of Union cavalry charges with an anecdotal cry from his men, 'Here come them fools again with their sabres. Give it to them!' If and when they reached the enemy, not every trooper could

actually use his weapon. Sabre work in close mêlée is a skill and it takes a comparatively long time to train a man in its use – records tell of many one-eared horses in the early volunteer regiments.

The tactical debate of side-arm versus sabre can be resolved by studying photographs of the cavalrymen. Many Union soldiers carry carbine, pistol and sabre, indicating a shared reliance, but the Confederates can sometimes 'bristle' with guns: a slung carbine, carried double-barrelled shotgun, a holstered pistol and another two thrust in the ammunition-pouch-laden belt and not a sabre to be seen. Indeed, Logan's Cavalry Brigade of 1864 was never issued with sabres, it was a highly mobile firing platform. The much improved efficiency and effectiveness of the mounted man's firearm caused a reversion to the tactical precepts of early seventeenth-century cavalry but modified them by remaining in close contact.

Although the cavalry was an important 'eyes and ears' force, cavalrymen were also employed as raiders. Whole cavalry campaigns were given over to rapidly striking at strategic points behind enemy lines, creating as much chaos and damage as possible and quickly getting away with any captured items before a response could be organised. Battlefield use was limited because of the firepower of the infantry but once in action against other cavalry, they were known to shoot and slog it out. In June 1863 at Brandy Station almost 20,000 cavalrymen were hotly engaged for nearly 12 hours, during 3 hours of which they were involved in continuous charges and countercharges along Fleetwood Hill.

In the early stages of the war, the artillery had the luxury of firing from long distance, well out of small arms range. Generals sought high ground for their echelon-set batteries to give covering fire and the ability to face another front. However, as the rifle replaced the smooth-bore musket, they began to be exposed and when the better rifles with 1,000-plus yd of maximum range came into mass production and issue, they were prime targets, especially for marksmen assigned to the 'duty' of wiping out the enemy gunners. Although in certain instances when massed to do a particular battlefield job (such as clearing the sunken road at Shiloh where they were packed hub to hub), a battery of guns usually deployed with approximately 14 yd between each piece, each gun being allowed 2 yd itself. This gave plenty of space to operate, being dispersed enough not to provide a dense target for counter-battery fire, yet also being near enough for battery control. A 6-gun battery occupied around 82 yd of frontage while a 4-gun one took 50 yd. Their transport limbers and horses would be deployed facing the enemy some 50 yd to the rear. They were near enough to effect the rapid removal of the guns but far enough back to require the enemy artillery to raise their elevation in order to hit them – it reduced the chances of being hit accidentally. The ammunition caissons and other supply wagons would be another 50 yd back from the limbers and so even more difficult to hit with a stray shot. In ideal circumstances these carriages, wagons and horses would be deployed on a reverse slope and out of the line of fire. If defending prepared ground, a ditch and earth bank would be

Marksmen were assigned to wipe out enemy gunners

Marksmen used rifles with accurate ranges of 1,000 yd plus. This conflict saw the first use of the telescopic sight

hurriedly constructed and range markers would be put out or, if coming directly into action, one gun was used to gauge maximum solid shot range before the battery commenced firing. Each battery carried 100 rounds; 75 per cent were solid shot or shrapnel, while shell and canister made up the rest. Orders to change from shot to shrapnel or shell were given according to target formation, and when the target was within 250 yd the switch to canister was ordered. At 100 yd a decision to run or fight on had to be made – after that there would be insufficient time to limber and get away. The caisson and limber teams would withdraw and the gunners then used double canister in a very bloody last ditch attempt to save themselves. Unlike infantry or cavalry, gunners, overrun in mêlée, tended to be butchered by infuriated and shell-shocked attackers.

One particular tactic employed by well-trained crews was to withdraw firing, which was achieved by three gunners carrying out the loading operations and the other six pulling on prolongues (long ropes attached to the gun). Well-drilled teams and crews could get a gun into action, unlimber, fire and relimber in under a minute, although accuracy was not a consideration. Most crews could get off 2 rounds per minute, 3 if they cast all care to the winds, but at Gettysburg, Hunt insisted his Union guns fired 1 round per minute as the optimum speed for efficiency and effectiveness.

To get range, gunners preferred rifled guns but, to do maximum damage, the smooth-bore was still the most efficient. This was because powerful, rifled guns tended to drive their explosive shells into the ground where their burst was severely curtailed and few splinters surfaced, except those which followed the entry path. General Imboden, seeing this phenomenon at Bull Run, somewhat rashly claimed a battery of smooth-bores was worth two of rifled artillery. They did not have the accuracy but at least they hurt when they hit. The rifling of a gun could also be damaged by firing case or canister, which the old smooth-bore did to perfection, especially, it was believed, the Napoleon.

No matter the type of weapon, the fighting men of the American Civil War were civilian soldiers rushed into service with weapons that could knock them over at ranges greater than many of their commanders were used to. Those men who had seen war before, had fought Indians or Mexicans whose firepower was not awesome. The percussion cap had made a tremendous difference to the reliability of the musket and the new rifling had extended its range. Breech-loaders and repeaters speeded up rates of fire and the newer machine-guns gave a taste of the awful power about to be unleashed upon other battlefields around the world. The American Civil War showed that two equally matched and proficient armies could do to each other with the new weapons. Unfortunately, the rest of the world dismissed it as a sideshow, which was to be to their cost.

THE COLONIAL WARS

THE COLONIAL WARS

The Industrial Revolution, which had engineered so many changes in manufacturing, focused its attention on world trade early in the 1800s. Global merchandising had always been a dream of merchants who saw the world as a vast resource to be used for the betterment of mankind in general and themselves in particular. Most European nations had private adventurers operating small trading companies all around the world, and the infant United States too began seeking inroads into the Spanish dominated Americas. Britain, France, Spain, Portugal and Holland vied for

Parade, drill and more drill

trade along the coasts of Africa and India and persistently moved into the lucrative spice islands and the East. The biggest trade war had centred upon India and finally that vast continent had come under the auspices of the British East India Company, who also ousted the Dutch from Sri Lanka. However, it was the technological leap forward that introduced the practical use of steam power to revolutionise transport on land and sea which enabled these companies to trade on a larger scale and over far wider global routes. Trade had to be protected. Investment was on a huge scale and the thought of such losses intolerable. National pride was stirred up and the expanding interests of the entrepreneurs became deliberately confused with national interests. Naturally these people looked to their mother country if they were threatened by indigenous natives or other aggressive competitors from other nations.

The modern industrial world came to their aid, with mass produced weapons, warfare, and the supply of nationally proud, adventuresome young men. Whether they were educated, born into the privileged classes and travelled POSH, or illiterate, slum-sweepings herded below decks, or fresh-faced young lieutenants in smartly tailored uniforms, or grim-visaged, hard-bitten cannon fodder in rough, ill-fitting tunics, they went to fight for Queen, Emperor, Country or Union. Whether they were British off to India or French going to North-East Africa, Americans pushing west, Dutch sailing for the East Indies, Belgians going up the Congo or Italians securing Africa's Mediterranean and Red Sea coasts, they were leaving their mother countries and taking both the dreams and means of global expansion with them. They took muskets, rifles and cannon, sabres, lances and bayonets and imposed their will, ways of life and laws upon peoples, countries and continents who had until then never seen a white man. First came the missionary, then trade, then the army. They undertook daring and self-

'Sons of Britannia'

sacrificing exploits to safeguard the financial interests of those who did not care if they lived or died, and, in doing so, helped destroy cultures and peoples while earning for themselves places of honour and pride in their own national consciousness. It was a curious age, when rapacious exploitation and mass murder were given patriotic veneers, and yet it witnessed some of the most amazing feats of military expertise and bravery. Small, technologically advanced armies, sometimes composed of both European and native troops, fought their way across, took and held vast tracts of land in the face of immeasurable odds and horrendous climatic conditions. It is easy today to say that the Martini Henry or the Snider had a bit of an advantage over the spear but it was sheer professionalism and raw courage that kept the soldiers in the line and gave them the ability to use the tools of their trade.

Britain was the leading nation in this period of Imperial expansion, and the age corresponds almost exactly with the reign of Queen Victoria. She came to the throne in 1837 as Queen of an important European country with a steady economy and trade links that reached out around the world. When she died in 1901, she was Queen Empress of the British Empire, possibly the most industrialised and rich national power to conquer, colonise and administer a huge proportion of the globe. Whether worldwide colonialism was right or wrong, it was a major feat. To create and hold such an empire took prodigious efforts and a lot of sacrifice, and it was held together by a network of military might – by a dedicated navy and army of sailors and soldiers who spent their lives aboard iron ships or in brick barracks, guarding or fighting for the Empire.

THE MEN

These 'Sons of Britannia' are often shown in drawings and paintings of the time as clean-cut, healthy young men, idealistic, patriotic and English, fighting for Queen, Country and the Church, with neat moustaches, shining boots and dazzling white equipment crossed over bright scarlet uniforms. But the reality was often different from the image. From early photographs dating as far back as the Crimean War of the 1850s, we frequently see that the British Empire was enforced by tired, prematurely aged men and women, doing what they, or others, saw as their duty, whether they were of European, Asian or African descent or were Christian, Budhist, Hindu, Jewish, Moslem, Sikh or of any other religion. The fighting men were often dirty and untidy, with bushy beards, holed boots, tea-stained equipment and sun-bleached, rust-red or dull khaki patched coats. Some books that tell of their deeds call them heroes led by demi-gods, while other describe them as thieves and murderers, led by imbeciles; that is all opinion. But what is fact, is that extraordinary things were achieved by ordinary people. People come in all shapes and sizes, are of all creeds and colours, and each has an individual character. It was this diverse collection that the British Army turned into a 'fighting machine' capable of carrying the Queen's laws and rule to all parts of her Empire. The army enlisted individuals from all around the world and from all walks of life and, by discipline, uniform, barrack life, comradeship, tradition, drill and punishment, created the Victorian Soldier.

The army constantly needed more men to replace those who retired, died of disease or were killed in fighting. Recruiting officers – often splendidly dressed sergeants or part-time pensioners, able to inspire, cajole or shame – toured cities, towns, villages and the countryside, put up posters, sounded trumpets, beat drums, bought beer and told extraordinary tales of adventure. They also bribed magistrates, drugged wine and told lies. From countries all over the world soldiers came, from all walks of life, and from all social backgrounds, although officers tended to come from the 'better off'. English soldiers were still the 'scum of the earth', sometimes enlisted as an alternative to prison, transportation or hanging, or to escape desperate poverty. There was no social security, and no welfare system; instead there was the workhouse, prostitution and the army. In other countries it was different; army service was often seen as an honest trade. In India, being a sepoy was worthy of both Brahmin and Shastri castes; badmashes of any caste or sweepers were not permitted. To a family in Nepal, acceptance into a Ghurka regiment was a great honour and a proudly guarded tradition. In Ireland, the potato famines and biting Atlantic winds were good recruiting officers; in England, it was Jack Frost. No matter if they were 'the sweepings of the gutters and prisons' or docile country boys brought up by honest parents, they were all usually deceived or enticed into the ranks by the scarlet coat, the promise of girls, grog and gold, and the prospect of promotion and fame. Rations, lodgings, clothing, education, travel and money were great temptations.

When men and boys took the Queen's Shilling, the deal was struck, the contract legal and they were soldiers for a period of at least twelve years. Brimming with pride, bribed with bounty, bullied by a judge, befuddled by beer, or overawed by the tales of an unscrupulous recruiting sergeant, recruits were rounded up and taken to a local depot to be recorded and to have a rudimentary medical check. Figures for recruits in Britain for 1884 tell us something about soldiers' backgrounds and the health of the country. Men of 'evil extract' or those who were sick or crippled were rejected.

	Percentage of all recruits	Percentage rejected
Labourers, husbandmen, & servants	54	46
Carpenters, smiths, masons, etc.	17	42
Clothworkers, weavers, lacemakers, etc.	14	48
Shopmen & clerks	7	41
Professionals & students	6	50
Boys from military schools	2	18

Of 10,000 enlisted, 6 per cent were described as well educated, 24.5 per cent could read and write and about 10 per cent could read but not write.

The 1st Battalion (57) Middlesex Regiment of the 1880s – the Diehards

The army constantly needed more men to replace those who retired, died of disease or were killed in battle

Taking 1865 as a typical year, line parties of sergeants etc. in 207 trawls brought in 6,179 approved men. Militia parties of pensioners etc. in 704 trawls brought in 4,265 approved men. These approved recruits marched to the nearest railway station, where they were loaded onto open cattle trucks and trundled away from their families to their new family and its home – the Regiment and its barracks.

Army barracks were often brick or stone, two- or three-storey buildings surrounding an open parade ground. (The old-fashioned prisons we see today are based on the design of these early army buildings.) Here, amid very strange surroundings, the reality of enlisting sunk in. Stripped, scrubbed and shorn, given a rough, ill-fitting uniform, uncomfortable boots and about a yard of hard bed space, the new recruit soon appreciated that he had left his old life behind for good. Whether he dreamed of the hills of Cork or New South Wales, the banks of Loch Lomond or the Ganges, a farm in Wiltshire or Kraal near Pietermaritzberg, his barracks was his nightmare before becoming his new home.

Living together is important in making soldiers part of a fighting team. They have to have undivided loyalty to each other, based upon friendship and habit. This was achieved in the barrack room. In Victorian times a barrack room was austere, often whitewashed and usually with beds down each side and a long table down the middle. It was bedroom, dining-room, lounge, hall, store cupboard, and utility room all in one. It was designed to house about twenty men but could hold more if the NCO ordered the beds to be moved closer together. Everything was done together. Reveille, or the wake-up call, was sounded on a trumpet or announced by a bell or a gun and came with a lot of shouting by corporals and sergeants early in the morning – about 5.30 a.m. The soldiers dressed quickly and made their beds, folding everything into neat piles and stacking it away; sometimes the beds were collapsible too. They set the central table with their eating and drinking utensils; in England, it was knife, fork, spoon, plate, bowl and mug. When all was 'correct' they were paraded and marched to the washhouse. Again usually about twenty at a time, they stripped to the waist, lined up at long slate sinks, put their enamel basins beneath a tap and washed, usually in cold water. Hot water could be found, but only a mug-full for shaving. Marched back, they redressed in their working uniform, cleaned their ablution kit (basin, razor, brush, soap dish, toothbrush) and stored it. A small group were marched to the cookhouse to collect breakfast, which was brought to the barrack room and dished out. With plates of food, hunks of bread and mugs of hot, strong, sweet tea, they sat and enjoyed their breakfast. Then it was clean it, store it and march out to drill or work. About midday, they marched back, washed, lunched, cleaned up, stored and marched back to work. About 6.00 p.m. they marched back for wash, dinner, clean up, store and then, unless they were on guard duty, they were allowed to amuse themselves in 'off duty time'.

The daily 'work' varied according to location. At the training barracks it meant drill. There was drill for everything, from simple facing in different directions on command and marching in perfect order, to complicated loading and firing movements, or intricate patterns of wheeling and counter-marching. Drill was often obsessive in most European armies, even the US had its fair share of martinets and parade ground soldiers. There was a belief that parade drill and ceremonial marches were the only training a soldier needed. Firing his weapon was a secondary consideration, and only those who had perfected the intricacies of drill were permitted to do anything with their gun except carry and clean it. It may be argued that many in the 24th were 'solid, steady shots from the old country', but it was noticed on Gingindhlovu that the British still had their Martinis sights set at 1,400 yd when the Zulus were at 300; the men did not know how to make maximum use of their own rifles. Training for battle was prescribed but it was often based upon practices of a bygone age. Fortunately, the correct stance and positions used in confronting an enemy when armed with a rifle and bayonet were in the drill manual; unfortunately, it did not mention the enemy often had a shield.

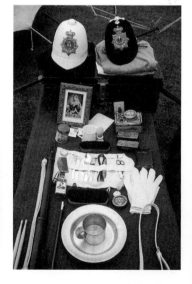

The Victorian soldier's kit

Other work was the operational duties of a garrison. The artillery were fortunate here, as they at least had gun practice that consumed shells and these had to be made. Routine was given over to the selection, measurement and filling of shells with gunpowder until all such firings were deemed too expensive and the men were all required, upon ignition of a piece, to yell 'Bang' instead. The next absorbing pastime of the military was cleaning – if it moved, salute it, if it didn't, clean it. Parade ground stones were painted and polished, equipment gleamed, coal buckets were clean enough to eat from and even the coal itself had a sparkling sheen. Pity the poor recruit who put polished coal on the barracks stove. Kit inspections, room inspections, weapon inspections, drill inspections; it was a round of mind-numbing tedium and pedantry. It did, however, turn the soldiers into a team, and a responsive one at that. It made for unquestioning obedience, pride in self and unit, and channelled all passionate, personal and violent feelings into a fury to be let loose in a mêlée with the enemy.

What Victorian soldiers did in the evenings depended very much on their social class, who they were, and where they were stationed. Prayer played an important part for many. Hindus went through their rituals, Moslems had teaching from the Koran, Christians held Bible lessons and everybody had lectures from their officers on the evils of drinking and drunkenness. Drink was popular, and canteens, where alcohol could be bought, were frequent additions to forts and barracks as they stopped soldiers disappearing into local towns and villages to get drunk and cause a nuisance to local people. Gin, and sometimes rum, was issued free in Britain and abroad because it was cheap, although the distribution of free rations did not last for the whole of the Victorian period. Indian troops were fond of bhang beer and arrak and the Sudanese were known to consume vast quantities of a local 'firewater'.

Gambling was also popular with card games and dice being the most common as the 'equipment' was small, although Chinese troops often set up full games of mah-jong. Soldiers had to sew and mend, and many became good at embroidery. Antique shops today sometimes have very beautiful silk tapestries featuring regimental names or numbers that were produced by men during the long evenings. Those who could read had newspapers and often found themselves reading to comrades who could not. Those who could write often wrote letters home for themselves or for friends who told them what to say. Soldiers everywhere sent messages, keepsakes and letters to their families and loved ones, unless they lived with them.

PASTIMES

Long periods in barracks, sometimes shut in during the midday heat, and long nights far away from home and family led soldiers into a vast selection of pastimes governed only by human ingenuity and social mores. Drinking was universal, until Temperance meetings discouraged and replaced the conviviality of the canteen for some. Telling tales, scaring new recruits with gory details, and nostalgic reminiscences filled many hours. A lot of men practised arts and crafts, and military museums boast splendid arrays of carved bone galleons, ivory statuettes, embroidered silk replicas of regimental colours and a plethora of other models and pieces of artwork produced in the cramped confines of a barrack-room or POW camp. Making their own entertainment was a prerequisite and playing musical instruments was popular, while even the 'musically challenged' joined in the singing, belting out choruses. The lonely harmonica accompanying the slowly drifting smoke as it meandered around a tent encampment was not as 'Hollywood' as some might think.

Gambling was a popular pastime

Some soldiers' families did live in the barracks. A blanket was hung around a small area to curtain them off for privacy, but their lives were just as public as the rest. Women and children, even small babies all shared. Who could have their family in depended on a long waiting list, and sometimes on the whim of the officers, who could be bribed with favours from the women, such as laundry. Women were allowed as long as they did not cause fights, but they often did, out of jealousy, or religious convictions. If a regiment was posted away, the wives drew lots to see who could go. Normally, two in twenty were permitted 'on the strength', which meant that they were counted as part of the force and drew rations and had space allocated to them aboard the transports. When the Victorian soldier sailed to another country – even in peacetime – it could be a very sad occasion as sometimes a posting would be for years. Some men had a family at home and one abroad. Marrying a local girl was not encouraged but it happened. Many Anglo-Indian and Anglo-Egyptian families come from these marriages. Men would get permission to leave the barracks two nights a week, or go to their homes outside the walls. Some abused the privilege, but while they were 'home' the army did not have to feed them. Barrack life was very public, it was not comfortable, but it was warm, dry and full of friends. Every necessity and even a few luxuries were provided, and those who did not want to never needed to go outside the garrison walls. It was a way of life designed to bind men together. It forced them into units, dictated friendship groups, and gave them the habit of being together and depending upon each other.

A soldier's daily rations in barracks in 1858 were the same as those fixed in 1813: 1 lb of best-second quality bread, and ¾ lb of ox beef or mutton and, on active service, 4 oz more meat. It was issued as raw meat inclusive of bone, and the size was radically reduced in cooking. An officer, commenting upon the diet of his men, said that sixteen were issued with 12 lb of meat, 3 lb of which was bone and much of the rest fat and gristle, so that 6 oz of 'meat' was a flattering amount of an individual's ¾-lb allowance. The men had to pay for this through stoppages before 1873, after which it was free but even then any potatoes or other vegetables had to be purchased by the men themselves and handed over to the cooks to prepare, cook and take their 'share', or else they had to pay 3*d* a day for having them provided. With few very rare exceptions, the only method of cooking was boiling in large 25-gallon cast-iron coppers, catering for thirty to forty men. Meat was brought from stores in a coded net indicating which barrack room it was for, and this was lowered into the pot to make a watery broth with pallid meat and floating grease. Every man took his turn as cook, so basic was the food to prepare. They used the same simple utensil for boiling coffee, tea and all washing water. Any food refuse, including peelings, was sold to a contractor, the money being used to put towards a Christmas dinner, unit cooking nets, or buying smocks for the cooks. A typical menu would consist of toast, cold fat skimmed off boiling meat, and coffee for breakfast; boiled mutton with boiled potatoes, cabbage and bread for dinner; then bread and 'fruit' jam with tea in the evening. The usual method of distributing a 'portion' was for each man to take it in turns to be 'carver' and to hack up the meat as best he could and call out 'who shall have this?'. The men, not seeing the portion, would call out their name and receive whatever was allotted, albeit only bone and fatty gristle – somebody had to have that portion and bad luck was not consistent. When two had to share one portion, one carved, the other chose.

NCOs fared better, and could run to a tablecloth with sergeants' mess cutlery and glasses instead of tin mugs. They sometimes shared the same kitchen as the men but food was served on proper serving dishes. A sergeant of 1870 recalls that breakfast was sausages, with unlimited bread and butter, fair coffee, milk and sugar; dinner was a nice soup, a round of beef, plenty of potatoes, boiled onions and cabbage; tea was copious quantities of ready-milked and sugared tea with generous bread and butter and a slice of fruit cake; and supper was bread, cheese, some raw onion and a glass of beer. Commissioned officers had very different fare and conformed to whatever were the nearest raw materials available, to proximate the tables of wealthy civilian Victorian gentry. No meal was complete without several courses and dinner was the main feature of the evening and not taken at midday. Some officers' messes were very rich, while others moderately so. However, in general, their mess bills were extortionate and a man without a private income of several hundred a year (thousands in the cavalry) could hardly aspire to remaining an officer. The artillery was reputed to be less fussy over meals but this was probably because the nature of their service made them a minority, or guests of an infantry or cavalry regiment. At Woolwich, such a claim would be ridiculous as their silver is renowned. No matter which service, a good mess was still the talk of any station, and most messes had an excellent cellar.

In general terms, the officers quaffed champagne, claret and brandy, while the men partook of beer and gin, but the variety was endless. Drinking alcohol was often the soldier's only relief from the tedium and appalling living conditions of the barracks. Each barracks had a canteen; some were cosy, almost like a civilian public house, while others had flagstone floors and a few rough tables and chairs. (However, not all canteens were 'wet'. From 1868 regulations set up 'dry' canteens as well.) On foreign stations, wide verandas around the outsides of buildings provided shelter from sun and monsoon rains, while a serving hatch communicated with the central storeroom. Although being drunk was a criminal offence, officialdom frequently turned a blind eye to it. In truth, there was very little they could do about it, and many regiments derived income from licensees operating the canteens; the more that was drunk the more profit the regiment shared. Early in the period, canteens stocked only spirits, cheap, poor quality, fierce stuff that soon had inbibers reeling. In 1847 parliament pressure on the army forced them to switch to beer only, although spirits could still be had very easily. It was only a measure to 'control' drinking that often got out of hand.

RELIGION

Being frequently in fear of imminent death, soldiers in wartime maintain they have a special relationship with their god, ranging from the devout to the bitter. In barracks there was rivalry and open hostility between religious groups, notably the 'Proddys' and the 'Pope's Boys' and other minorities were sometimes picked on for being 'different'. While not excusing the awful things that went on in the name of religion, soldiers tended to place more emphasis upon how a man behaved, especially under fire, and upon how he conformed to what the army and his mates expected of him rather than what religion he followed. Being of a particular faith was, at times, a unifying factor and public pressure made worship a regular and public event. In the British Army 'Church of England' was the officially accepted religion and men had to attend church parade; being a Non-conformist, Catholic, Jew or a member of any other creed, brought dispensation so long as the men made 'alternative arrangements'. Many did so with visiting ministers, rabbis, priests or elders. However, in India those 'let off God-bothering' joined the charpoy cult. As armies encountered other religions, they ridiculed them until time and understanding brought these creeds acceptance in a wide pantheon of gods. Native troops did much to increase the colonial soldier's appreciation of other religions, as he watched 'different' men go to their gods with the same steadfast courage and resolution to do their duty as he hoped he would show when he went to his.

It would be wrong to give the impression that all soldiers were drunkards. Temperance societies had existed within the army since 1823, while Gregson's Regimental Temperance Association was founded in 1862. By 1885, there were 144 societies with 12,231 members in India alone. By 1896 that figure had risen to 22,810, with a further 12,119 at home. However, it has to be said that copious amounts of booze, beer or bhang made some men susceptible to taking offence and becoming argumentative and downright violent. The resulting bar-room brawls were a release mechanism for all the pent-up anger and frustration they endured as 'Victorian' soldiers. Inspired by Kipling's poem 'Gentlemen Rankers', Donald Featherstone's work on the life of these men notes that, apart from snatches of exhausted sleep, alcohol was the only way for a man to forget that he had placed himself in what was found by some to be an intolerable situation – a situation where every waking moment was at the whim of someone in a superior position, who could sadistically make his life a misery or, at best, keep him on his toes in a world of barked commands, implicit discipline and harsh punishment for offences and omissions. Inter-regimental rivalry was a mainstay of the British Army but it did lead to ferocious barrack town fights between men the worse for drink and armed with belts, broken bottles, cudgels and bayonets. Staggering pay nights so that antagonistic regiments were not out on the town together was one quick solution; another was the provost martial team, wielding pickaxe handles.

In parts of the world where alcohol was forbidden by religious law, the soldiers' canteens were off limits to those who would find it offensive. Devout Moslems were horrified by the drinking behaviour but others soon caught the habit, if not so dramatically or publicly. It was because of the European soldier's reputation for uncontrollable drinking that, during the Bengal Sepoy Rebellion of 1857, a known battle tactic was to leave stolen and opened casks of spirit or bottles of beer at points of attack, meant to distract and break order. Sometimes it worked. No matter how they got hold of it, many soldiers of the expanding trading empires spent a large proportion of their pay on alcohol. Others were more responsible; encouraged by regimental savings banks, they retained their money for the day in the future when they would be discharged.

The first money a recruit received for his years of service and the risk of life and limb was 1s – although that could buy a considerable amount in the 1800s. Many also received an enlistment bounty, which increased during wartime. At the beginning of the Crimean War, this was £7 15s 6d, but by 1885 it had risen to £10. The war being over, in 1859 it dropped to 2s 6d upon enlisting, 7s 6d on approving, and £2 10s on joining the regiment – a total of £3. In the 1860s it had gone down to just £1 – the same amount paid to any European serving in India to transfer to the new incoming regiment if his own was going home to England. Standard pay was 1s a day plus the 1d a day 1800 beer money allowance, but stoppages for clothing, food and equipment reduced this by about half. There were also stoppages

for breakages, damage to uniform, and contributions to other more obscure regimental funds to pay for soap, boot blacking, etc., as well as the pay sergeant's 'fiddles' or delaying tactics that could result in men's pay being six months in arrears, although happily this was no longer the case by the 1870s. During wars, when casualties and foreign diseases reduced the strength, delays were more common as dead men's pay was shared out by certain unscrupulous officers and NCOs, who also falsified the books and changed dates of death etc. to boost their profits. In 1847 it was ordered that no soldier was ever to get less than 1*d* a day actual cash. In 1845 good conduct pay was introduced at the rate of 1*d* a day for every seven years' exemplary service and in 1854 stoppages were reduced from 6*d* to 4½*d* a day. However, the influence of the Great Duke was still strong throughout the century and he always argued to keep soldiers' pay minimal and the expense of the army low to keep the country happy. To pay more, the House of Commons reasoned, was to give soldiers licence to drink more and, under that influence, they would commit more crime, which would necessitate more harsh punishments – thus combining reactionary and liberal concerns in one argument. Sir William Robertson, who joined in 1877 as a trooper, considered himself lucky to have 5*d* a day left.

In 1867 army pay was reviewed. It was decreed that every recruit was to receive 'a complete kit of necessaries free of charge, as a single issue, to be kept up by him at his own expense'. Every man in the cavalry was also entitled to a Bible and a Prayer Book if he could read and knew to ask for them. However, Trooper Mole of the 14th Hussars found his 'free kit' did not include his whip, dandy brush, sponge, burnisher and walking out cap and consequently had 14*s* 3*d* deducted from his bounty. Basic pay also went up. It was argued that even agricultural labourers, traditionally the lowest paid workers in society, earned more than private soldiers, troopers or gunners. A 1*d* a day basic increase was approved. By 1870, the 1806 long service pay and the 1845 good conduct pay systems were reviewed and awards were restructured, amalgamated and payments made, along with a badge (a stripe sewn on the sleeve). The money was calculated in years of excellent behaviour with no record of punishment:

Years of Good Service	Extra Pay per Day	No. of Badges
2	1d	1
6	2d	2
12	3d	3
18	4d	4
23	5d	5
28	6d	6

There were also Good Conduct and Long Service medals, with a gratuity of £5, and a Meritorious Service Medal for NCOs with an annuity of £20. Bravery too was rewarded with an increase of pension. In November 1901 Henry Wilson D.A.A.G. of Pall Mall wrote to the author's great-

Above, left: Cloth and cork helmet with the white cover for foreign service; above, right: The Glengarry cap.

grandfather to inform him that his son, No. 5373 Lance Corporal F. Scott, had been awarded the Distinguished Conduct Medal for 'conspicuous gallantry in assisting a wounded officer under heavy fire in bringing up ammunition to the firing line' and that the DCM made him 'eligible for an extra 6*d* per day to his pension if recommended on discharge'. The recommendation was very important because one incident of drunkenness, insolence, petty theft or anything deemed misconduct and a soldier lost the lot – years 'clocked up', extra pay, badges and pension. The army pay book had a special page for recording misdemeanours so that they could be pay-related.

Increases naturally also accompanied promotion, but so too did workloads, responsibilities and isolation from friends. To become a Non-Commissioned Officer, a private had to pass a First Class Education Certificate to prove he was proficient in reading, writing and arithmetic. It was usual for an educated enlisted man to be promoted early, within two years, to the unpaid (pre-1878) rank of lance corporal where he might serve a three-year probation period until promoted to corporal and a basic daily rate of 1*s* 7½*d*. To make sergeant, he had to pass a Second Class Certificate, which examined difficult arithmetic, fractions, and the balancing of various accounts. As a sergeant he received 2*s* 6*d* a day and a copy of the Regulations, Instructions, etc., for which he paid 3*s* immediately. The number of sergeants deemed necessary for the good running of a battalion often exceeded the number deemed necessary for economic prudence, so those who acquired the rank were frequently overworked for their increase. Probably the most onerous duty was orderly-sergeant, undertaken on a rota and for one week at a stretch. They were on duty 24 hours a day, never leaving the barracks, sleeping fully dressed in the guard room and at the beck and call of every incident and officer's whim. However, special duties for NCOs carried additional pay, so the men took on more work to keep up with the demands made upon their purses. Naturally, all rates of pay were higher in the cavalry, but so too were the expenses.

Army uniforms are a study in their own right, but the intention behind them has always been to dress soldiers smartly, which adds an impressive and imposing air to their appearance, yet to do so in a style that does not encumber their strenuous actions and fighting ability. During the colonial period, training and manoeuvres were often public occasions and the distinction between the dress of the parade ground and that of the battlefield became somewhat blurred. Lines of men in shakos with brass-pointed helmets, scarlet, blue or green coats with white crossbelts and cartridge boxes supporting haversacks and bayonet were seen on Horse Guards, the Champs de Mars and the plains and hills of foreign countries.

Early British colonial troops wore the French-style shakos, which changed shape with fashion, going through a series of increasingly silly designs. Prussian influences produced the more conical look and then the classical, cloth-covered, cork helmet, the shape of which is retained by

EDUCATION

It was seldom thought necessary for a soldier to be educated and even Napoleonic officers had little schooling. Le Marchant, who did much to found Sandhurst, and other reformers pioneered the teaching of officers so they could better understand their duties. Then for many years the British Artillery and Engineer arms led the world in teaching both its officers and men reading, writing and arithmetic in order to study books on their crafts and do the necessary calculations involved. Academies and schools were set up and other countries followed suit – one of the most notable being West Point in the USA. It was many years before armies took an interest in the education of the 'cannon fodder'; they equated literate men with trouble-making barrack-room lawyers. Once again late nineteenth-century social reformers had a hand in bettering the soldier's lot with volunteer classes and a range of unofficial medals and proficiency certificates, and a literate man in the barracks of a foreign posting was a godsend for receiving news from home; he was always high on the 'sippers list'.

As armies grew in size, and organisation became more complicated, written regulations multiplied, and administration duties demanded NCOs were literate. Lessons and tests were brought in to ensure thay could function. The establishment of an Education Corps in the European and US military was the next step in bringing all soldiers up to a basic standard, capable of reading drill books and manuals. Then, as trades became more technical, so entrance tests were developed and branches such as Signals made greater demands of recruits and promoted Further and Higher Education courses for them. Armies are keen to point out that they are no longer the refuge of the illiterate and unemployable.

British policemen today. For foreign service it was made in white, and early versions had a khaki cover, but later it was issued in khaki drill. For undress, the men wore a variety of pillbox hats, with or without peaks, or a soft for'an-aft cap called the Glengarry. During Victoria's reign, British soldiers also officially had two types of what we would call a jacket. The first was the general purpose, 'brick-red', wool frock coat. It was unshaped and unlined, with wool reinforcements over the collar and cuffs in the regimental facing colour, and it was usually fastened by brass buttons. This was the most commonly worn garment for daily parade, work and fighting. On special occasions the tunic would be worn. This was shorter, tighter and tailored to a waisted look, often in better quality wool and sometimes lined, especially for officers. On campaign they wore the same wool frock coat but a regiment sent to a garrison in a hot climate such as India often had cheap cotton uniforms sanctioned. Official trousers were dark blue serge wool with a welted seam and often were worn tucked into black leather gaiters or the tops of service issue boots. The army boot was still uncomfortable and not waterproof and the men tried all sorts of 'dodges' to make them easier to wear without looking different, such as fleece-lining a size too big, and working in grease and fat to soften the hard, cheap leather. The box pack was a heavy crippling thing to wear. It contained all the soldier's necessaries, his few luxuries, and was a trial to contend with. It went out of use in the 1860s, replaced by the 'valise'.

The new repeating weapons meant that each soldier had to carry a good supply of ammunition and a system was designed and later modified by Slade that incorporated two ammunition pouches onto the arrangement of belts which carried the valise. (From the 1860s ammunition pouches were carried on a waist belt.) A more uncomfortable piece of army equipment has yet to be devised – the weight of the cartridges pulled on the shoulders, which were already taking the weight of the valise. The new weapons also prompted a change in the colour of most army uniforms around the world. Men in bright colours with target-enhancing crossbelts were easily seen and aimed at by accurate long-range weapons, so a less obvious dress was necessary. Armies chose more natural colours, sandy yellow, olive green, duck blue, etc., while the British chose khaki, first achieved by dyeing campaign issue cotton whites in tea.

Although all arms changed easily to the more camouflaged look, the cavalry retained a distinctive and individual appearance where they could. The lancers retained the plastron-fronted tailored look in both coat and coatee, and only wore the 'cork helmet' instead of the czapka on campaign late in the period. They kept their riding boots and breeches, and adopted Indian jodhpurs to add to their different apparel. The mounted infantry were even allowed jodhpurs but had puttees, another Indian 'acquisition', rather than boots.

THEIR WEAPONS

From 1816 to 1860 there were major improvements in small arms. Ignition by flintlock was superseded in military use around 1840 by the percussion system, which was simpler and easier to use than the complicated 'art' of

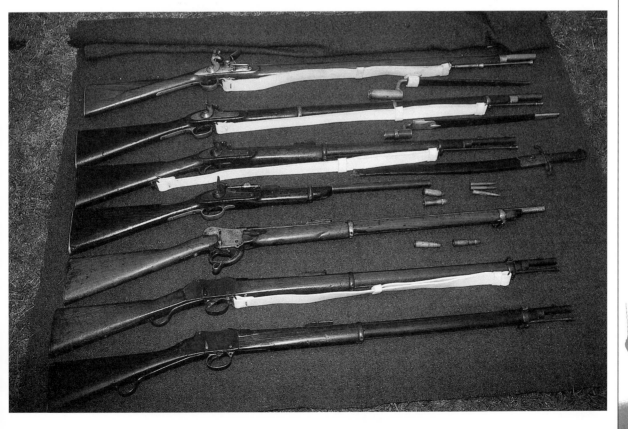

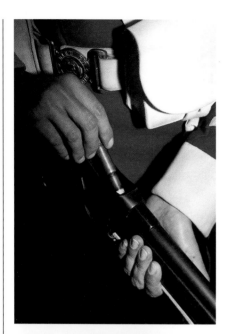

Left: Cartridge being inserted into breech; above: Cartridge being pushed home with the thumb; below, left and right: after pushing the lever down from the stock, the cartridge is ejected after firing

setting a flint, and it was also more reliable, especially in rain or windy conditions as there was no open pan. In the 1850s Minie developed a precision rifling tool that rendered the smooth-bore obsolete and enabled nations to arm their men with accurate firepower weapons. Meanwhile, industrial processes speeded up and mass production methods reduced costs and made it possible to equip large numbers of troops rapidly with the newer, more deadly rifle. The American Civil War was a testing ground and the armies of the world watched and noted how various weapons performed and how well new inventions fared, such as the hand-cranked machine-gun. They learnt from its technological advances but not its appalling effects. The result of this was that from 1865 to 1913, the technology race that was developing in the world of weaponry speeded up because the prototypes had been tried. To be a few years behind in the race was to put a nation's soldiers at a considerable disadvantage. The biggest breakthrough was the perfection of the metallic-cased cartridge, which made repeating actions possible and led to the magazine rifle, the machine-gun and the quick-firing field gun.

Rifles: The principal weapon of the European colonial armies and the American drive west was the rifle. Problems in design, which led to a slow rate of fire, were overcome with the introduction of the breech-loading system, which freed a soldier from laboriously thrusting a greased patch or cartridge down the muzzle against the rifling grooves. The notion of breech-loading is almost as old as guns themselves; Henry VIII owned a breech-loader in the sixteenth century. Early military mass production began in Prussia with the Dreyse, which opened and closed the breech with a bolt action but it ignited the charge via a needle-like firing pin passing through the powder charge to strike the fulminate in the base of the bullet. The central exploding ignition and the paper cartridges did nothing to help prevent escaping gases and the breech often blew, making the men fire from the hip rather than steady an aimed shot. In 1866 the French adopted the Chassepot, which also used the needle firing system but this time it struck a percussion cap at the base of the cartridge, which increased its efficiency, and a better engineered action helped limit gas escapes. One of the most revolutionary inventions was the Pauly cartridge, which, for the first time, combined ignition point, priming, charge and projectile in one paper-enclosed unit that could be thrust into the breech of a rifle. The Lefaucheux paper case used the same brass base but with a pin-fire primer; but it was the Boxer cartridge designed for use in the British Snider rifle of 1867 that combined all these innovations. Boxer devised the lead bullet slotted into a coiled, thin brass case set upon an iron base with an improved centre-fire power. When struck hard in the centre of the base the primer would explode, ignite the charge and propel the bullet, while the brass case helped seal the breech and prevent force dissipation. This did away with the percussion system and allowed the hammer itself to do the work. It was the mass production of metallic cartridges that enabled the breech-loader to begin its take-over and, by 1879, it was the standard infantry weapon of most European armies.

Once reloading via the breech had been perfected, it was now made mechanical and a wealth of single-shot rifles were produced. In the Martini action, pushing down a lever to the rear of the trigger lowered the front of the breech block and cocked the firing pin inside it. The soldier thumbed a cartridge down and forward into the chamber and then raised the block into position by pulling the lever back to the stock. By squeezing the trigger, the firing pin was released off its cock and shot forward to strike the centre of the cartridge. In action at close range, the Martini-Henry bullet was observed passing through seven Zulu warriors before becoming embedded in an eighth; it was also noticed bouncing off a Zulu shield at 100 yd. But the Martini had problems. It had a savage recoil, which often left the shoulder bruised. It fouled quickly and the case of the Boxer

cartridge sometimes grew too hot and expanded. The tin base parted company with the case when hot, causing it to jam in the breech and necessitating digging out with a metal lever of some description. However, most of these early breech-loaders suffered similarly.

Model	Effective (yd)	Calibre (in)	Weight (lb)	Length (in)
Dreyse Needle	700			
Enfield & Enfield-Snider 1867	900	.57	8¾	39
Remington Rolling Block 1871				
Chassepot Modele 1866	500	.4		
Le Gras 1874				
Martini-Henry 1871	1,450	.45	8½	49½
Springfield Model 1873				
Mauser 1874				

Once breech-loading had been perfected, it opened the way for the development of efficient repeaters. Hand loading was fast but sometimes, as noted, the brass case jammed in the breech when it grew hot. The next move was to design a mechanism that expelled the spent case every time, so another armature added to the lever pushed the smoking case out of the breech as it lowered the block. However, an even better solution was to have the spent case expelled by the insertion of a new cartridge, and to have this done mechanically, and repeatedly. This was the theory behind the perfection of the repeater. These weapons depended upon the loading of a number of cartridges into a form of stored magazine, into the base of which was fitted a strong spring to push them along a pathway towards the chamber. They were fed into the chamber itself by a hand mechanism. In the Winchester action, working a lever under the stock and pivoted forward of the trigger slid the breech block back, releasing the spent case. This simultaneously dropped the chamber into line with the tubular magazine set under the barrel, where the magazine spring forced the next cartridge back and into place. The lever was then pulled up, bringing the chamber back in line with the barrel, sliding the breech block forward and in behind it and re-cocking the hammer ready for the trigger to be squeezed and the round to be fired. The repeater replaced the single-shot breech-loader as soon as it could be mass produced in sufficient numbers to equip armies.

Model	Calibre (in/mm)	No. in mag	Range (yd)	Weight (lb/oz)
Colt Lightning slide action 1885	.44 in			
Henry	.44 in			
Vetterli Model 1881	10.4 mm	13		
Mauser Model 1884	11 mm	8	2,200	
Lebel 1886	.315 in	8		
Lee-Metford 1888	.303 in	8 then 10	2,500	9 lb 8 oz
Krag-Jorgensen 1889	8 mm	5		

Bayonets: The twisting socket system of fixing was gradually replaced by a vertical sliding socket and the shape of the blade changed from the triangular cross-section to the sword blade type that could be used in a slashing action as well as for thrusting. The Field Exercise manual of 1867 shows both types in use, differing according to use with the long or short rifle. The earlier type, designed to be used as a massed anti-cavalry weapon in place of the pike, proved too restricting in the more personal man-to-man combat. The new type gave them the thrusting reach of a stabbing spear and the cutting edge of a sword.

Bayonets were used in both attack and defence. Unlike during the American Civil War, most charges in the Colonial period were intended to come to grips with the enemy. They were often performed in open order to lessen any casualties from fire and entered into with bloodthirsty ferocity. No matter the nationality, the men constructed a cherished myth of their proficiency with the cold steel, the success of their charge and the enemy's dislike of ''avin' it up 'em!'

Model	Weight (lb/oz)	Length (in)
Enfield Socket	13½ oz	17
Enfield Sword	1 lb 12 oz	23
Martini-Henry Socket	15 oz	21½
Martini-Henry Sword	1 lb 12 oz	23
Lee-Metford Sword	1 lb ½ oz	12½

Machine-guns: The rapid firing of early machine-guns led to many problems, especially the feed system, often by gravity from a hopper, that could jam because of skewed cartridges. They also suffered from metal expansion problems caused by the sheer number of explosions and firings they undertook. The 'fit' of the cartridge in the chamber became slack and the case twisted and caught, or it became too tight and gripped the case – again the result was that the gun jammed and hand cranking did not produce sufficient force to free it. In 1884 Hiram Maxim produced the fully automatic machine-gun, which harnessed some of the energy of the exploding charge to power the operating cycle, replaced human strength and human ability to operate the mechanism quickly. It was first used by the British in 1888 in Gambia. Many nations and manufacturers copied the Maxim and made improvements. Three of these important innovations led to recoil operation, belt feeding and water cooling, which made the machine-gun the standard, if not the essential piece of infantry support weaponry. The chart below gives some information about the most popular of the many that have been produced.

Model	Usual no. of barrels	Cyclic rate (per min)	Range (yd)
Gatling 1865	6	300	1,200
Gardner 1874	2	120	900
Maxim 1890	1	600	1,000
Montigny Mitrailleuse 1870	37	370	900
Nordenfelt 1873	3	350	900

The Gardner had two sliding breech block barrels, in line and 3 cm apart. Cartridges were fed down a slotted feed lane by hand and a manually turned crank opened each breech alternately for the round to drop into the chamber. As the breech block slid back in place it struck and fired the cartridge. In 1882 the British Army bought both the two-barrel and the newer five-barrel models. However, the Maxim was the 'star' of the machine-guns. When cold, and firing in short bursts, it could deliver up to 1,000 rounds per minute. Many men came to fear the 'chatter' of the machine-guns, so much so that the Mahdi told his men that Allah would silence them when they attacked. God is not so obliging with military miracles, especially when time and money have been poured into alleviating jamming problems.

Artillery: From 1865 to 1914 rapid advances in efficiency and design were evident in the big guns too. In 1858 the French adopted rifled barrelled artillery and after the American Civil War other nations followed suit. By the 1870s, breech-loading persisted, although problems with escaping gases were not solved until Armstrong evolved the leather obturator ring to seal the breech. The major problem to solve with artillery was how to combine the speed and ease of reloading the breech-loader with the power efficiency of the muzzle-loader. The escape of propellant gases from an ill-sealed breech caused loss of propulsion force, dangerous jets of burning gas, poisonous fumes in enclosed spaces such as casemates or turrets, and the risk of the chamber splitting or shattering. As the use of guns was becoming widespread inside forts or positions dug into the earth, where space was at a premium and muzzle-loading therefore impractical, a solution had to be found. In fact, two solutions emerged. The first was the 'Quick Firing' system, which used a brass case to the cartridge. This was forced so tightly against the inside of the barrel that no gas could leak back. The other was the De Bange system, which employed a mushroom shaped piece behind the charge and a soft (leather) ring between it and the breech block. The force of the explosion acted upon the mushroom piece, forcing it into the obturator, which in turn was squeezed out hard against the barrel walls, forming a seal. Once this problem was solved, the mechanism of closing the breech was worked upon and fell into two camps, the sliding block, which suited the QF system, or the screw breech, which favoured the De Bange. The quickest and most effective was found to be the interrupted screw mechanism, whose cutaways through the thread enabled the breech block to be secured with just a turn through several degrees.

New and more powerful explosives were also introduced. Melinite and Lyddite both enhanced the destructive power of the shells and greatly increased the blast circle for shrapnel. Better fuses too were developed, which made a greater range possible. The chart opposite lists several of the most popular guns frequently deployed in the great land grabs of the nineteenth century:

Model	Rounds (per min)	Range (yd)
French 75 mm Cannon Model 1897	20–30	
37 mm Pom Pom QF	30	2,750
Krupp 75 mm	2	6,000 with shrapnel
12-pdr RBL	1–2	3,800 with shrapnel
15-pdr RBL	1–2	4,100 with shrapnel
12-pdr Naval	1–2	7,000 with shrapnel or HE
4.7 QF Naval Gun	1–2	10,000 with shrapnel or HE
Creusot Long Tom 155 mm	1	11,000 with HE
5 in Howitzer	1	5,000 HE shell
2.5 1877 RML 7-pdr Mountain gun	1	3,300 with shrapnel
		4,000 with HE

In most European armies, a battery consisted of 6 guns and 6 ammunition wagons, 1 store wagon and another replacement limber also carrying stores, 1 forage wagon, 1 water cart and 1 cavalry spring cart.

Each gun had enough ammunition to keep it in action for about 3 hours of continuous fire, or a day's more usual fighting. This consisted of:

13-pdr 30 common shells, 108 shrapnel shells, 4 case shots, 133 star shots
16-pdr 24 common shells, 72 shrapnel shells, 4 case shots, 133 star shells

When depleted they had to send back to depot for stores to issue more from their campaign reserve allocation:

13-pdr 333 common shells, 120 shrapnel shells, 46 case shots
16-pdr 120 common shells, 144 shrapnel shells, 8 case shots

There were also many different types of siege and naval guns of all ages, makes and nationalities in use around the world throughout the period.

THEIR FIGHTING

For much of the expansionist period, fighting methods were based on struggles between unequal sides – European technical supremacy versus indigenous native numerical strength. Courage being equal, it was the weapons that gave the advantage. The Europeans had to keep the native troops at a distance so they could use their superior firepower. Once they closed, the hand-held cutting, jabbing and slashing weapons often proved more than a match for the bayonet. Coupled with a shield used offensively, as practised by the Zulus, then the result was often a foregone conclusion. Numbers, too, often dictated the day, especially if the native leaders were prepared to take the initial losses among their men. Early musket-armed parties of European troops were able to shoot down an advancing front rank with two or three well-controlled volleys, but were unable to reload quickly enough to get off further rounds. They were soon overrun and despatched. However, rifling gave greater range and breech-loaders had higher rates of fire and were generally more accurate, which changed the situation quite radically.

In European theatres of war, the idea of deploying men in neat lines and advancing across open fields was doing nothing more than presenting the enemy with excellent targets. At St Privat, the Prussian Guard lost 8,000 men in 20 minutes to a line of Frenchmen armed with Chassepot rifles. But, as many European and American expeditionary forces seldom encountered troops with anything remotely akin to their own weaponry, this tactic remained in favour as it meant discipline and control. The 'line' was synonymous with military prestige, honour and power and to be part of it was a measure of bravery and manhood. Natives, armed with spears or knobkerries, could be knocked down several hundred yards away, long before their own weapons came into play. Even those with muzzle-loading matchlocks, jezails or copied Tower flintlocks were no real threat to the men carrying the Martini-Henry, Mauser, Legras or Springfield. However, the firepower had to be mutually supported and ammunition supply had to be smooth and efficient. At Isandlwana the companies were spread so far apart that their fire could not support each other. When they also had problems with ammunition supply, their fate was sealed, but not before they had inflicted horrendous casualties on the assegai-bearing Zulus.

However, if they had ideal conditions to meet it, European troops stood a good chance of halting a native charge. Howard Whitehouse charts a Hadendowa charge over open ground against a company of 100 fresh, steady, European troops:

Long range:	1,400 to 700 yd 7 mins fire @ 6 rounds per min. 2% effective = 84 hit
Medium range :	300 to 700 yd 4 mins fire @ 6 rounds per min. 5% effective = 120 hit
Close range:	100 to 300 yd 2 mins fire @ 6 rounds per min. 10% effective = 120 hit
	(rate also reduced to allow for time to fit bayonet)
Point Blank:	0 to 100 yd 30 secs fire @ 10 rounds per min. 15% effective = 75 hit

Virtually 400 casualties in 12½ minutes. Risk not fitting bayonets and it rises to nearly 500. Whitehouse also points out that the volume of fire was as important as the number of hits in deterring an assault. A company in a two-deep close order line would have a 40-yd front; at 600 rounds per minute a fire volume of 15 shots per yd per minute could be achieved – 1 shot into every foot of front every 12 seconds. That should be enough to stop any crowd of advancing opposition.

Sometimes the tribesmen would be armed with similar weapons rather than the various forms of spears, bows, axes, knives and swords. A Nyamwezi chief boasted 20,000 men armed with guns, but the weapons were very old and unreliable, including Berber muskets and large number of Tower Brown Bess flintlocks sold to him by unscrupulous traders. Military historians tend to make too much of native troops and captured armaments. The Zulus did have Martini-Henrys after Isandlwana, and the Mahdists had plenty of Egyptian equipment including Remington Rolling-blocks after the 1883 crushing of Hicks Pasha, but they lacked ammunition and skilled men to use them. The greater fear for the men and their commanders were the profiteers. Arms dealers are nothing new and, while they put money in their pockets, the soldiers of the late nineteenth century had to face the weapons they sold. The American western film often depicts the gun-runner with a case or two of ex-army rifles secreted in an old wagon being traded to the Indians, but this is small-scale stuff compared to the entrepreneurs of the colonial powers. During the 1890s Menelik acquired 25,000 rifles from French and Russian sources; and, by the time the Italians faced him at Adowa, he had re-equipped with 80,000 modern rifles including those from Martini, Gras, Lebel, and Remington, some of which he had bought from Italian companies. Native craftsmen too were often excellent copiers, and industrial spies kept them up to date with new developments. Samouri Toure first used copy-Chassepots, re-equipped with copy-Gras and finally his workshops produced enough copy-Kropatschek repeaters to re-issue for a third time.

Despite the increased range and rate, one recurrent problem the men faced was that of battlefield smoke. The powder produced volumes of thick, choking grey smoke that quickly enveloped the line and prevented soldiers

At 600 rounds per minute a fire volume of 15 shots per yard per minute could be achieved

from seeing and thus aiming at their target. Some tacticians argued that volley fire, although less accurate and less efficient than independent fire, at least gave any breeze a chance to clear the blinding smoke between volleys. Volleys also meant more disciplined and soldierly behaviour. Independent firing could dissolve into frantic and wild firing that could quickly consume the private soldier's 60 rounds in less than 5 minutes. In the Sudan, Macdonald ordered his officers to issue his native troops with 3 rounds per man to stop them firing off too much ammunition, and Kitchener, at Omdurman, is reputed to have ridden down the line crying 'Cease fire! You do not know how much this is costing!'

The general tactic of the line had not changed very dramatically, despite the increased proficiency of the weapons. The idea was still to advance in close or open order under fire, until about 800 yd from the target and then deliver slow, regular volley after volley to weaken the opposition. This was done by alternating ranks of fire. The front rank would advance about 5 yd from the second line, halt, fire and then kneel to reload. The second rank would then fire over the heads of the front rank and then advance through them, kneeling to reload about 5 yd in front. The first rank would then stand up and fire and pass through themselves. This rolling fire would continue until they came to about 50 yd and generally would have suppressed the enemy fire. The line closed, doubled files into single line and

a charge with the bayonet was made to put the enemy to flight or to give them the 'cold steel'. Sadly, the long-range effectiveness of this tactic can be deduced from Count Gleichen's figures as he records that, although marksmen could pick off delineated targets at 1,800 yd, most regular soldiers could hardly hit a thing over 450 yd. However, as the range lessened, the accuracy increased, massed shot effect had an influence and casualties were caused. Losses to an enemy with greatly inferior firepower were usually negligible, except at very close range when they had to remain steady in the face of a bayonet charge if they wished to fire. The Boers were probably the best equipped army a European force had to face and accounts tell how they too suddenly lost accuracy and experienced a fall in numbers firing when the charge swept up a hillside.

No matter the range, the introduction of the magazine and the repeating rifle meant that intense and devastating firepower could be brought to bear at particular points and times. Improvements to machine-guns, notably water-cooling and recoil-operating, produced a rate of over 1,000 rounds per minute at a range of over 1,000 yd. This led to them dictating tactics, especially when lightweight versions (the Maxim only weighed 60 lb) could be carried to intransigent native strongholds and used to suppress any enemy fire or resistance until the infantry went in. The famous 7-pdr screw guns could also blow them out. Massed riflemen and machine-gun crews could lay down fields of fire from which nothing much could expect to emerge unscathed. The defensive square, with its all-round fire and morale-boosting nature, made a comeback, but this time with battalion machine-guns covering the weak corners and vulnerable only to long-range rifles or artillery, which the enemy did not have. Mercifully, such amounts of firing soon produced the battlefield blanket of thick grey-white smoke that enshrouded men and terrain features alike, preventing each side from seeing the other. In such circumstances, the barked commands of the NCOs took over. Veterans of several engagements and knowledgeable of various native tactics, they would call sight settings and organise volley firings, while their men just obeyed.

The development of smokeless powder, such as the propellant cordite in 1892, meant the battlefield no longer became wreathed in grey. Targets were visible at greater ranges and for much longer. The repeater magazine, combined with the ability to see a lot more, meant that the counter-attack was now a real possibility. Men could adopt open order, load in cover and then fire a covering shot to move, reloading as they ran and working their way towards a position that did not disappear into a fog bank. In defence too this worked in favour of the colonial powers. The firing effect of 100 men armed with the Martini-Henry charted earlier should now be recalculated using Lee Metfords opening up at 2,000 yd, with increased percentage efficiency and a much faster rate of fire. In ideal conditions, they could literally mow down any attack. Support them with Maxims and the natives have little chance. Commence with long-range HE from the guns and shift to case as they close and they are annihilated.

Yet smokeless powder also meant that a concealed enemy could remain hidden. This was of little concern when facing untrained and unskilled natives using captured weapons but, in the hands of skilled men, familiar with their own rifles, the bloody lessons of the American War of Independence had to learnt anew. Berber, Afghan or Boer positions in rocks were not disclosed by puffs of lingering smoke; the enemy's bullets came from nowhere and left only the dead or wounded for evidence of their presence. The tactics shifted once again to deadly games of hide and seek among the rocky outcrops, dunes and dongas of Africa, and India. Long-range duels evolved between marksmen, while those not trained or accustomed to such work found themselves either standing or crouching in line, waiting for the wild bayonet charge, or marching endless flanking miles to turn a position.

The bayonet charge was fast disappearing from battlefields where both sides had modern rifles, but against enemies who could not lay down fire, the rush with the 'cold steel' had a revival. European troops were never short of discipline and aggression, which were essential elements of the bayonet charge. After suppressing any fire, the infantry would fix nearly 2 ft of razor-sharp knife to the end of their rifle and sprint forward to thrust it into an enemy's body. Coming to hand-to-hand fighting had a mixed reception. Fode Sila's men ran from the charge of the West Indian Regiment in 1894, while the Zulus considered it more manly than the shooting war. The Sikhs met it head-on and exchanged skill in the intricate parry and thrust of bayonet and spear fighting, while the Boers thought it 'brutal and unchristian' and often surrendered in the face of it. It showed a certain naïvety to shoot down men up to a few feet away and then hoist one's arms and hope for clemency. The Boer tactic of raising a white flag to induce the British to stand up and then opening up on them from close range with a party who were 'unaware' of the surrender, or declaring the person who raised it had no right to do so, or that they had changed their minds, did nothing to encourage the ordinary soldier to show restraint once the order to go in with the bayonet had been given. The bayonet charge had one thing over the firefight. It was decisive. It confirmed victory and moral superiority. An enemy falling back under heavy fire can rationalise the move as a withdrawal, but a foe thrown back by the bayonet knows it has been defeated.

According to the military manuals, the successful strategy was always deemed to be the attack. Moves would be simple and in such formations as could concentrate firepower. Scouts would be flung out in all directions to detect any attempts to ambush or encircle and they relied on tried and tested simple tactics. The Europeans maintained that native troops, and indeed Boers, seldom had good security, especially at night when scouting also went by the board. A rapid night advance and a dawn attack was described in all the officers' handbooks. This was often to be coupled with a feint attack from one direction to mask the real thrust. If an attack was not easily accomplished, then the major ploy was to resort to provoking the enemy into attacking across open ground onto prepared positions, using skirmishers to draw them into a fire trap. Preparations would include digging rifle pits, creating thorny zaribas, building stone sangars, throwing up barricades of stores or laagering wagons; even kneeling camels would suffice. These defences offered protection from fire but, more importantly, broke the impetus of a native charge, which was their main tactical advantage. Getting natives to squander their advantage was not always difficult.

This is where cavalry and artillery came into play. Horse soldiers could still move faster than most native armies on foot, so it was often their job to raid and draw attention to themselves, riding into range, firing and then running away. Hopefully, this would entice a chase and, depending on the numbers involved, would result in another squadron shooting their pursuers down with their carbines or drawing them onto the rifles of the column. Artillery also could be used to provoke by lobbing long-range shells into a camp, town or packed mass and then switching to their usual role of infantry support when the attack came. The guns used in colonial warfare varied from huge naval guns, mounted on special carriages and towed across country by teams of oxen, or even elephants, to small

mountain guns that broke down quickly for transportation on the backs of five mules. Horses, however, remained the standard means of getting the guns into action throughout the period, and these teams and crews deployed in very much the same fashion as they had done for the previous one hundred years. Each gun of a 6-gun battery was 20 yd apart, with its limber about 20 yd to the rear. A further 20 yd on the crew horses were stationed, and 20 yd beyond that were the ammunition wagons. They were not as dispersed as the Americans had been in the 1860s, but the 100-yd front and 100-yd depth fitted neatly into a parade ground and made drill movements easier to control and coordinate.

Although methods of fighting varied, there were several general points of consensus. These included getting the guns up close to the enemy to cause as many casualties as possible and to have a bad effect on their morale. Long-range shelling of an enemy position was thought detrimental to a successful battle as it often caused a withdrawal, and the guns were there to destroy the enemy not drive him off. The only time bombardment was advocated was to silence enemy artillery covering the area of an attack. This was artillery as infantry support, and performing this role was not always easy. When they pushed the guns foward, the gunners often came under small arms fire; Col Long brought his guns forward at Colenso only to watch his men shot down by Boers using their long-range rifles. Neither

was it easy to support infantry at long range, because when the army changed into khaki, spotting could be confused; British guns at Spion Kop failed to provide artillery support as they believed the Boers on the slopes were British troops.

Because of the power of the rifle, cavalry charges were rare, although they did remain firmly set in the minds of the officers. A French, old-fashioned, massed cavalry charge was quickly broken up by the Prussians at Worth. Against native infantry their outcomes were also uncertain. Stewart's Hussars at El Teb and the 21st Lancers at Omdurman both encountered hundreds of swordsmen willing to fight them, while the Chasseurs d'Afrique had to be rescued by infantry at R'Fakha in 1908 after they had broken through the Moroccan line. The boot-to-boot, hell-for-leather charge was still a warrior's version of fox hunting. The theory stated that cavalry were to scout, pursue and dismount to fight with their carbines, but they often ignored that for the 'glorious' charge.

The basic tactics of the charge had changed little from the Napoleonic days with its three divisions of assault, support and reserve troops. Even at Balaclava, when whole regiments were assigned these tasks, the same sequence of events unfolded. Commencing with the 'walk-march' at 60 to 80 yd a minute, the squadrons move slowly forward, keeping order and

control over the first half of the charge, sometimes more than half a mile. About 800 yd from the enemy, they moved up to the 'advance', going at the trot of 120 to 160 yd a minute to gather momentum. At 300 yd they would increase speed to the canter of 180 yd per minute, which pumped adrenalin through rider and horse. Finally, at 100 yd, they would spur into the 'swinging gallop' of up to 240 yd a minute. Lances or sabres would be lowered, yells would come from their throats, and man and beast would launch themselves into the enemy line, shattering order on impact and dissolving the fighting front into a confused mess of hacking and slashing. Meanwhile, at 200 yd, the supports would swing outwards and charge into the mêlée, often from the flank; their impetus and arrival often proved sufficient to decide the fight. Having broken the enemy, the reserves would come through and pursue, while the assault and support troops rallied. Ill-disciplined cavalry tended to ignore this latter essential part of the tactic and joined the pursuit. They might have won their sector or taken out their opposite number but, being totally out of control, the force became useless for further action. At Aliwal, the steady discipline of the 16th Lancers enabled them to make charge after charge and, in doing so, make a significant winning contribution to the course of the whole battle.

Cavalry could not often win battles but they were the major element in defeating enemy troops. The Egyptian Campaign was drawn to a rapid close because of the relentless pursuit of the British and Indian cavalry, covering 76 miles in 36 hours. The cavalry did not give the Zulus any opportunity to regroup after Ulundi as they harassed them into the hills, burnt their kraals and kept driving them further and further apart. At Elandslaagte, the 21st Lancers rode through the retreating Boers several times, picking them off their horses and wagons with their lances. This caused great indignation, as the Boers felt that they should be allowed to retreat and reform in safety; ignoring the prime military role of their enemy's cavalry cost them dear.

Left: To be effective and produce the desired force of penetration, the lance has to be used at a gallop or, at the very least, a canter. At close quarters the sabre was the preferred weapon

Right: In 1836 bamboo was chosen as the best material for the lance. Originally, they were made of oiled ash, but it was discovered that these warped in warm climates. Lance pennons of the national colours were fixed just below the steel point

Below: The success of Napoleon's Polish Lancers caused other countries to equip their own cavalry with the light and manoeuvrable 3 metre spears

Training for war often became a sport. 'Tent-pegging', or spearing a tent peg hammered into the ground, called for precision work with the point and a forceful thrust

The 'Death's Head' was the 'Death or Glory' symbol of the British 17th Lancers

Left and centre: The Lancer in full dress uniform

Right: The undress uniform was used for walking out and everyday wear, although not when doing 'stables'

Left: The Cavalry Carbine was shorter than the Infantry Rifle and therefore easier to handle in the saddle

Centre: Left flank

Right: Right flank

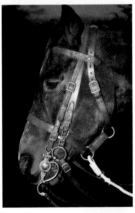

Left: Bridle

Centre: Right flank rear of saddle

Right: Right flank front of saddle

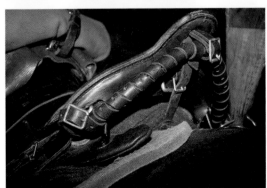

Left flank rear of saddle

The Electric Telegraph. This became the standard communication, even connecting Europe to Africa, using Morse Code, invented by the American electrician S.F.B. Morse. The code comprises a series of dots and dashes, or short and long signals, relayed by a simple on/off switch or key. Each letter of the alphabet is represented by a short sequence of dots and dashes

The Heliograph. On a cloudless day, using the sun's rays reflected from a hinged mirror, it was possible to send messages up to 90 miles using the British 14.137 in model or 48 miles using the 7.087 in model. At its peak of efficiency, it was possible to send messages of up to sixteen words per minute. Oil lamps with magnifying lenses were also used, but with less effect

Semaphore. Flags were used to convey messages, but were only of use over a limited distance, and were prone to visibility problems, even with the best telescopes to view them

Each arm had its tactical role to play in a battle. The cavalry found the enemy and, by manoeuvring, pinned them to a position. The artillery then softened them up and kept them away from the infantry, while they, in turn, hurt them and broke them. The cavalry took over again to pursue and destroy them. As each arm had it role, so each man had his job, and all was done in the name of God, Queen, Country and Regiment. With virtually unmatchable weaponry, unshakeable moral fortitude and fundamental raw courage, these men, no matter what hindsight makes of their ethics, captured the globe.

THE FIRST WORLD WAR

THE FIRST WORLD WAR

During the age of global expansion European nations were seldom at war with each other. From the fall of Napoleon until the emergence of Prussia as a driving force behind the unification of Germany, there had been various internal struggles, especially in 1848, dubbed the Year of Revolutions, but they were of little interest to the rest of Europe, apart from the profiteering from arms dealing. However, the German wars against Denmark, Austria and then France fascinated the rest of Europe as their military experts studied the new weapons and tactics and tried to interpret what their influence would be upon their own armies. Until 1914 most other nations contented themselves with foreign 'adventures', taking conflict to distant parts of the world in pursuit of trade advantage and Empire building. They used their modern weaponry on native populations in an unequal struggle for power and colonies. In these conflicts, the idea of the small professional army made up of veteran soldiers once again took hold and the citizen armies of Revolutionary France and the American Civil War were deemed things of the past so, when enmity between France and Germany over Alsace and Lorraine looked as if it might escalate into yet another German war, most countries thought it would be another brief, sharp, short encounter. What the military pundits of the day had not taken into account was national consciousness, and the true power of modern weaponry.

The infantryman's rifle could fire up to 15 rounds per minute, and machine-guns about 600 per minute. This hail of high velocity lead swept through a whole generation of men

Commercial and colonial rivalry between Britain and Germany was intense. Indeed, rivalries and old scores were behind a series of mutual protection pacts that the politicians created in the early 1900s. Gradually, armament and training programmes were begun and there was a desperate arms race in the building of Dreadnought battleships. German naval officers toasted '*Der Tag!*' – the day! – the day they would meet the British Navy in battle and defeat it, while French cavalrymen wrote letters to newspapers exalting the nation to remember the glorious charges of Jena and Wagram when the Prussians fell to their sabres, jingoistically boasting it would be ever thus. The clouds of war gathered and 'the spark in the Balkans' caused general mobilisation. Without too much delay, Europe plunged itself willingly into a full-scale internecine war, which nationalistically they had 'looked forward to with relish'.

With the outbreak of hostilities in 1914, automatic weapons, big guns and excellent small arms like the Lee Enfield, in the hands of professionals soon made their presence felt. Advances were brought to a sudden halt in a barrage of shells and a hail of bullets, and graveyards soon filled. The casualties were so great that the need for more men quickly became apparent. Large influxes were needed if the numbers at the front were to be maintained and, even more, if a breakthrough reserve was to be established. The demand for arms was also great and civil engineering factories were inspected as potential arms producers. At the front, the new weapons were too much for the strategy and tactics of the senior commands and both sides went to ground in the swathe of trench systems, forward machine-gun nests and long-range artillery batteries. Each time an attack was attempted, it was mown down or blown apart. It was not going to be a short, sharp war and certainly not over by Christmas 1914.

Through the newspapers and the infant film newsreels, it was also obvious that the civilian populations were in full agreement with complete mobilisation. The result was a return to citizen armies as the men flocked to the recruiting stations, driven by sentiment, jingoism and the dream of championing a just cause. The factories geared themselves to war, steel workers forged artillery barrels not girders, the mines produced vast stockpiles of coal, and the shipping industries began laying the keels of more warships. The professional élites were bleeding to death, so citizen armies returned to take up the fallen rifles and soon they were supported by whole nations in arms. The nature of warfare had changed yet again.

The losses were staggering on both sides. By 1915 the infantryman's rifle could fire 15 rounds per minute, the machine-guns about 600, while artillery guns could fire shrapnel-loaded, spread-effect shells at 20 rounds per minute. The 16th Baden Reserve spent four months in the trenches around Ypres and, according to one survivor, Adolph Hitler, lost 2,989 men out of 3,600. In July 1916 the 1st Newfoundland Regiment began an attack and ceased to exist in a matter of minutes. The whole pace of war speeded up and the sheer scale of the casualties was beyond comprehension. The increasing number of deaths in wartime is made even more terrible when one considers that the army's real killer up to this point – disease – had been reduced to a negligible proportion because of improved medicine and health care; these deaths were caused by weapons, including the indiscriminate use of gas. Nations in arms had no real effect upon winning wars, other than making them more efficient at bleeding each other dry.

To end the stalemate, the high commands tried the strategic game of opening another front to divert attention, men and materials. It came to no good as, in Gallipoli, the Allied forces ran into the same networks of wire and prepared defences as they encountered in northern France. They tried fleet actions, but they proved unrewarding in many respects, especially financial – the Dreadnought arms race, which had consumed so much money and energy, had created two equal forces capable of destroying each other from 20 miles apart for no significant gain. New weapons were tried. Gas was unreliable and subject to windage. Tanks, although effective, were prone to break down and could not be manufactured in sufficient numbers. Bombers were too underpowered to carry a worthwhile number of bombs. The artillery pounded everything from a distance, machine-guns dominated No Man's Land and the men hid from them both.

By 1917, France had lost a million men and, after the disastrous Champagne offensive, over half its infantry divisions sat in their trenches and refused to attack anymore. It was not a mutiny but rather a strike against tactics that offered them near certainty of death or maiming for no gain. The same year, the Italian Army practically gave up as it too had lost over a million men in just eleven months of its Alpine struggle against the Austrians. The Russian Army downed weapons as well and marched home despite the efforts of its officers. Only Britain and Germany seemed determined to slog it out. Nations in arms had produced a change at last – the war of attrition. Generals seriously calculated the ability of populations to sustain casualties and proposed maintaining the status quo in the way of waging the war, because, as Britain had a higher male population than Germany, in the end she would win.

Eventually, both these armies also tired of the war. Then in 1918 the Americans arrived. They were fresh to the battlefield and so was their nation to the war. It disheartened the Germans even further. By November 1918, the German high command had sufficient evidence to prove that they had got everything they could from their troops. Faced with the Americans and the futility of resisting, with troops too tired and too war weary to fight, they sued for peace and accepted humiliating terms at the Treaty of Versailles. Both sides had fought their men too hard, driven them until it had all become too much to bear.

In 1914 men had flocked to their armies in search of glory and victories, but then several long years of sustained conflict broke their will to fight. No real outcome appeared possible, and there were no great successes to cheer – only unending terror and drudgery. The citizen armies of the First World War were not the choice, hardened band of veterans able to bear privations with toughened, wiry bodies and sardonic humour. They encompassed men from all classes and all walks of life. The nation in arms produces an army of ordinary people in uniform, and ordinary people do not make natural soldiers, especially ones able to fight a modern war. John Keegan states that the philosophy that every man is a soldier rests on a fundamental misunderstanding of the potential of human nature. The men who fought from 1914 to 1918 took everything war could throw at them, bearing the brunt of the best of modern weapon technology and enduring the inflexible, hidebound dogma of their senior officers in the field and the uncritical and unsympathetic zealotry of the civilian population at home. They stuck it for as long as they mentally and physically could, which was far longer than could ever have been expected. Eventually they just caved in.

THE MEN

The first men to fight in the First World War were the regulars. The nations deployed their standing armies in the field in August 1914 and these were trained soldiers, able and fit, who had chosen the military as a way of life. Some officers and men were veterans of colonial campaigns, especially the Anglo-Boer

The men of the First World War were at first the preferred 'regulars'

War and, indeed, some of the oldest senior commanders had seen service as teenagers in the last European engagements of the Franco-Prussian War, some forty-plus years earlier. These were armies of experts, armed with the long-range, fast-firing weapons of the new century but led by brave yet bewildered men brought up on old-fashioned drill books. Ordered to undertake the tactics of a previous age with the weapons of the new era, they slaughtered each other with professional efficiency. The need for more men was soon realised and volunteer programmes were hastily put into place to persuade, cajole and shame men into joining up. It was a difficult task, because to be a soldier was

The high casualty rate meant a constant flow of new men was required

still to be a social outcast, a 'no-good character' with nothing else to offer except a willingness to submit to boredom, privation and death.

This changed with the recruitment drives undertaken by every country involved. Soldiers were now the saviours of the hour, the patriots, the brave and the good; the cult of the uniform was revived, with walking-out dress for soldiers on leave, and 'perks' for soldiers back from the front. One self-proclaimed 'patriotic recruiter' was Lord Kitchener, who quickly saw the need for men, whom this new technology would consume. He estimated that Britain needed 100,000 men as an immediate response to the war and his 'Your Country Needs You' posters, featuring himself pointing an accusing finger, appeared virtually overnight. All sorts of means were employed to get men to enlist. At a northern football match, the Lord Mayor made an address over the loadspeaker system and 149 men rushed to join, with a further 51 men responding to a second plea from the Mayoress. They were given red, white and blue ribbons as the crowd sang 'It's a Long Way to Tipperary'. The Government made a promise that if groups of friends, or 'pals', signed up together, they would not be separated for the duration of their service. Small groups of friends, sports teams and pub regulars joined, then villages, streets, factories or towns all flocked in together, to fight together and, more often than not, to die together. So great was this localised recruitment that whole battalions were formed from quite small areas and their nicknames, such as 'The Bradford Pals', testify to the success of the policy. It was to prove devastating to the civilian population when a 'pals battalion' suffered high casualties.

Even this was not enough for the hungry maw of modern war. Mass conscription became the order of the day. Boys lying about their age were not questioned too closely, those previously declared unfit were miraculously re-appraised in A1 physical condition and enlisted. The nation in arms had arrived, and the army transformed into a sprawling mass of civilians in uniforms, given guns and taught the rudimentary skills required to kill their enemies. Every new soldier underwent recruit training, in which he was taught the basics of handling his rifle, and then progressed to 'trained soldier training', during which he was taught to shoot, including grouping, application, snap and rapid fire. Deemed most important was the 'mad minute' of rapid fire, in which he had to get at least 15 shots inside a 2 ft circular target at a range of 300 yd. After completing this course, he went for 'field firing training', learning to shoot from trenches, from behind cover and when under fire himself. This training programme, prescribed in 1908, looks efficient until the cartridge issue is taken into account – about 300 rounds per man, per year.

Recruits came from every social class and after those deemed suitable as officers had been creamed off, the rest were thrown into the mêlée of general or specialised enlistment and regimental allocation. Men from one town found themselves serving in a county regiment from a distant part of the country. Travel was not commonplace in the early twentieth century and the first thing new soldiers had to do was to understand the 'foreign' accents of their NCO. They had to become accustomed to army life with its emphasis upon drill, discipline and denial. They also had to adjust to being in that great leveller, uniform.

The First World War saw the last of the rash of nineteenth-century cosmetic changes to soldiers' uniforms. Fashions had varied the headgear almost every decade and Indian and African service had taught the lesson of subdued colours and the adoption of khaki-dyed clothing. However, the basic format of jacket and trousers remained the same, although the crossbelts had given way to the Mills webbing system. The jacket of khaki serge hung to the top of the thighs and was secured by polished buttons and a waist belt. It was described frequently as tight-collared, although this was soft and turned down. The flapping trousers were held against the legs by another Indian innovation, puttees, long strips of khaki cloth bandaged around the lower leg and overlapping the top of the short leather boot. They took time and effort to 'get right' and be comfortable. The headwear was also in khaki serge – a stiff 'cheese-cutter' peaked cap that was replaced universally in 1916 by the steel helmet. Packs were still worn and they were still too heavy. The boots were still uncomfortable and in no way waterproof. Socks were thick, knitted and retained both heat and moisture easily. To add to this, each man was later issued with another piece of essential kit, the gas mask.

At the beginning of the war, very few troops wore any armour at all. The French cavalry retained their Napoleonic classical comb helmets and the

With the professionals falling at such a terrible rate, the Army soon became a Citizen's Army, full of young inexperienced men spurred into Army life by patriotic fervour

Recruits came from every social class. They all had to adjust to being in that great leveller, uniform

Webbing system

The First World War soldier, pre-1916, in battle order

Bayonet scabbard and entrenching tool handle

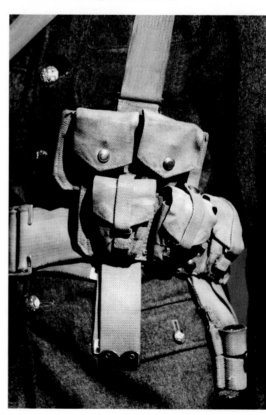

Cartridge pockets

Puttees were first used in India; the trouser legs below the knees were bound with long strips of cloth that overlapped the tops of the short boots. The boots were often of inferior quality, literally falling apart after a few months

Khaki serge 'cheese-cutter' peaked cap, replaced in 1916 by the steel helmet

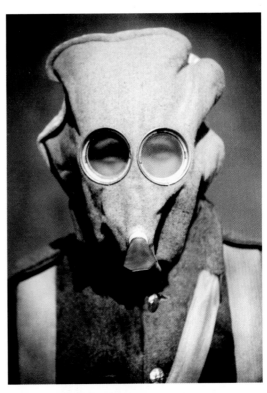

The gas mask. Wearing one of these made it virtually impossible to operate as a fighting man. They became unbearably hot, the eye glasses became heavily misted and were difficult to keep in front of the eyes

German infantry wore the *pickelhaube* helmet, but it was made of hardened leather and afforded only minimal protection, certainly none against bullets or shrapnel splinters. Most other nations issued soft caps to their men. After the opening phases of the conflict had settled into the dogged business of trench warfare, the disproportionate number of head wounds caused such concern that the French introduced a metal helmet, a variation on their civilian fire service helmet. The other countries followed their lead, the British issuing one like a late medieval kettlehat and the Germans a style very similar in appearance to a medieval sallet with a peak. By 1916, all soldiers at the front had been issued with helmets, although they did not always wear them.

As the conflict progressed, so other forms of armour reappeared, including the breastplate and pauldrons, which were given to snipers and some gun crews, who even got tassets – a form of leg armour. Others had special jackets with large 'pockets' into which pieces of armour plate could be dropped. This steel was thick and heavy and very tempting to remove but on occasions it could and did stop bullets, even artillery shrapnel.

Tank crews received a curious visor-like leather-covered steel face protector with a hanging mail front piece to cover the jaw and throat. Some marksmen pushed a small, wheeled and loop-holed steel pavises forward, while others wore a full headpiece similar in design to a closed helm. Although the authorities looked back in time for medieval solutions to protection problems, modern bullets were not as easily deflected or bounced as arrows, so the weight and thickness required to foil them made the wearing of the kit arduous and, at times, self-defeating, and useless equipment has always had a habit of 'getting lost'. To counter this unfortunate trend, deductions from pay were made for lost items.

The men's pay was not much better than their Victorian forerunners had received, although ration stoppages had disappeared and a lot more clothing was free issue. Extra pay for passing different proficiency tests had been introduced and it was not unknown for a soldier to get up to 15*s* a week, although his civilian counterpart often received 42*s*, or £2 2*s*. The Treasury argued that 'all found' was worth the difference, although few who stayed at the 'King's Hotel' or dined at the 'Khaki Canteen' would have agreed. Accommodation had been dramatically improved by the Cardwell Army Reforms of the 1880s but barracks were still spartan by early twentieth-century standards. They were usually built in two- or three-storey blocks with two rooms on each floor, one either side of a wide central staircase and each housing fifty men. It was supposedly one company per floor with NCO, mess servant and company stores accommodation included, but this was not adhered to strictly, especially when company and battalion strengths varied according to recruiting success and internal regimental policy concerning company allocation.

The men's rooms were obviously communal, with a row of beds, steel wall-lockers and chests down each long side of the room. The beds were

Pay for the soldier could reach 15s a week. His civilian counterpart often earned 42s (£2 2s)

iron and sometimes telescopic, sliding back to give more daytime space. There was usually a fireplace or a stove and the more senior men had the beds nearest to it. Like the Victorian soldier, the Edwardian kept his rifle in a rack next to his bed. He had one long or two square-shaped straw-stuffed coir mattresses, four blankets in winter and three in summer. Most regiments did not supply sheets or pillowcases but left it to the individual soldier to acquire his own if he wanted them – although they had to be hidden in his kitbag or personal chest for inspection as they were not

Command stayed firmly in the hands of the rich, the aristocracy and the well educated. These men were often promoted to command battalions above the veteran NCOs and experienced junior officers

'regulation'. Inspections were the same formal laying out of clothing and equipment that had dominated the soldier's life fifty years earlier, the only difference was that at least now he could no longer be flogged for the wilful disobedience implied in a wrinkled blanket, or a missing button stick.

Two barrack blocks faced each other across a parade ground and were linked on a third side by regimental offices, wash and cookhouses, laundries and stores, on top of which often ran another accommodation floor. All three buildings were sometimes linked by 'veranda walkways' with cast-iron spiral staircases. On the fourth side of the square were the officers' quarters, unconnected and set back slightly with a formal garden. This was a building of similar size, but designed to house not 300 but about 50 men with office accommodation, a large dining-room, library and smoking lounge, special kitchens and servant lodgings. The officers' rooms were furnished according to the individual's taste and purse and only a newcomer or a 'pauper' (a man with only a small private income) would use regimental equipment or furniture.

Quite a number of men could read and were encouraged to do so, as they could then read instruction manuals, drill books and technical training publications. They often had access to a library, although their moral welfare was looked after by careful monitoring of what was on offer. Dickens was still felt to be lightweight fare. Public houses were still popular venues for recreation and many situated close to barracks doubled as brothels. The Temperance Movement was growing in strength and soldiers' welfare was a concern, especially when every man was a soldier and a voter, and his wife had a special interest in how he behaved and where he spent his pay when not on home leave. Most men spent their meagre pay quickly. The fear of imminent death did little to encourage saving, although some had their money stopped and sent home regular payments to their wives and mothers. Records exist of admonishments to officers who did not immediately stop these payments from soldiers killed in action; the argument was that pay should cease the day before a man was killed because he would not have completed a full day's service on the day that he was killed and he was thereby not entitled to any pay for that day.

Officers usually came from the upper classes of all nations. These were those bred to be the leaders of society, and as such became the leaders in war. Influential individuals were given commissions to raise battalions and a 'middling sort of rank' within them for doing so, but command stayed firmly in the hands of the rich, the aristocracy and the well educated. It was assumed that they could do the job and that a good education and the team-spirit of the sports field imbued them with all the correct qualities to do it well. Regimental COs took on Battalion COs who were personal friends, relatives or even from the Old School House, rather than promoting experienced junior regular officers or even veteran NCOs. The British Army was like British society, class-riven to the point of idiocy.

The German Army was less class dominated than its French and British counterparts, but it too suffered from obsession with the protocol and birthright inherent in command. This marked a return to the idea of the social élite as the warrior class. Unfortunately, it missed the point that the old family ancestors had been trained in arms, had served in wars from boyhood, and knew what they were doing when they attained command. The Americans too had their share of old money and good families commanding regiments, but their approach to discipline made it far easier for those in that position to acquire the advice and guidance of their more experienced inferior officers. To the British, to seek such a thing would be 'bad form', and to receive it, if unsolicited, 'damned impertinence'.

Most officers brought their own horses to the front. Although the army did have a peace establishment of so many thousand horses, it was not enough. The Army Horse Reserve was formed and owners were paid a retainer of £4 pa and accepted a free veterinary service and inspection every six months, in exchange for the right of the army to requisition their horses within forty-eight hours if war was declared in Europe. By 4 August 1914, the artillery's allocation of 10,000 had been rounded up and they still wanted more. Horses were used by every branch of the army. Petrol-driven automobiles were used but they did not replace the horse. Transport relied on horses and wagons, pack mules and even pony carts. The guns were pulled by teams of horses and the cavalry required thousands of them. This modern army was still dependent upon the transport and movement system of medieval armies, although the men would have put up a case for considering they had returned to the Roman ways of Marius' Mules.

However, for all its faults, these armies were efficient in themselves. Even as citizens in uniform, they behaved well and performed with heroism and military proficiency the difficult, sometimes suicidal tasks they were set. Not every officer was a buffoon, some were outstanding and even Haig has his admirers among military historians. Some officers inspired the men with such confidence that they really did believe it would all be over by Christmas and the volunteers went off to war with a cheery wave, expecting to repeat the success of the Sudan and the North-west Frontier. On the first Christmas Day of the war, an unofficial truce was entered into by both sides along some sections of the line. Small gifts were exchanged, drinks swapped, several international football matches played.

On Boxing Day the shooting resumed and the men huddled in their trenches once more. Trench sizes varied according to their function, terrain and the ground itself. A common type was about 8 ft deep and 6 ft wide, with a firing step that enabled the men to rest their arms on the lip but still have protection from a small additional parapet a rifle's length forward. Early trenches were just cut into the earth but soon sandbags, logs, 'wriggly tin', debris and all other types of material were used to consolidate them. Some sandbags were even filled with a concrete-like mixture but this should not be confused with preservation and reconstruction edifices such as those on Vimy Ridge. They were cut in either a crenallated or zigzagged pattern, which afforded a degree of crossfire and usually consisted of four or five parallels linked every few hundred yards by zigzagging communication trenches. The advanced line was not usually complete but consisted of forward saps to short sniper trenches, observation posts and dummy lines, dug to draw enemy artillery fire. Behind this, at 50 yd, came the main front line and between this substantial emplacement and its second line of supervision trenches, another 20 yd back, was a warren of short connecting trenches, shelters and forward supply and command posts. About 150 yd behind this came the support trenches, fall-back positions and places where the men of an attack could await orders to go up into the front line in relative safety. A further 300 yd back came the reserve lines, where reinforcements could wait, and supplies move laterally across the front.

The communication trenches then ran out into the land behind the lines until they reached the comparative safety of the dead zone, where entrenching was considered impractical, not unnecessary. Dotted sporadically throughout the system were 'strong points', fortified emplacements containing several machine-guns or even a small gun or trench mortar.

Along the front of each line and covering the flanks of the communication trenches were entanglements of barbed wire. Modern farm barbed wire is nasty enough but military wire was even more vicious. It came in various forms with wicked barbs or razor-sharp, saw-toothed edges. Some 'wires' were nailed to posts and covered areas 20 ft thick and 8 ft high, while others were simply coils thrown out along a length. Getting through them was difficult for those who created them – the more complex were maze-like with passageways, twists and U-turns. To an attacking force it was impossible.

Living conditions in the trenches were appalling. They were damp, cold and uncomfortable. Men slept where they could, often in bunk-beds carved out of the wall of a dugout with only a blanket for warmth. The lucky ones had mattresses, taken from the wrecks of villages, or bundles of cloth made up from curtains and carpets. Washing and shaving was a luxury, although orders promulgating that men would be judged by their smart, clean appearance do exist. The men were often verminous, and lice bred rapidly in the dark, fetid regions of their underclothes. Delousing stations were set up behind the lines, where a hot flat-iron passed over their clothes supposedly killed their 'little visitors'.

The trench system

A strong point in the trench system, containing a Vickers machine-gun

Rations were sporadic and arrived when enemy bombardment and the mud permitted. Large field kitchens tried to keep up with demand and local bakers were put on full twenty-four hour baking duties every day of the week. Tinned food was produced in vast quantities. For the British, preserved corned beef (from the 'corns' (grains) of salt used in the brine for preservation) became a popular dish. This was known as 'bully beef', and being ready cooked it could be eaten cold or the tin pierced with a bayonet and immersed in boiling water for several minutes to warm it through. Tea, milk and sugar would be added to the residue of greasy water and tin mugs dipped in for a 'brew'. A tin of warm bully, a steaming mug of sweet char with a hunk of freshish bread was a meal fit for king . . . and the tins were useful too. They kept the water out, the food fresh and did away with plates and bowls. They could double as mugs afterwards and were even strung on string across paths in the wire to rattle together whenever an unsuspecting person came through.

Soldiers' letters throughout time complain of duties and life in the siege trenches but those of the First World War are more potent because, coming from an age of greater literacy, we learn the details of everyday life and its arduous round of work and fighting. There was always digging,

Barbed wire entanglements were placed in front of each line and on the flanks of the communication trenches

consolidation and repairing and, after bombardment or an attack, body clearing. Men's bodies blown to pieces by the big shells were hard to gather up and it was a depressing and disturbing task. Burial parties often had to be ordered to the gruesome job.

To stop themselves going mad from the tedious routine of manual labour, the endless bombardment of the enemy guns, and the sights and sounds of dead and dying comrades, the men of all nationalities had only songs, banter, cards and letters. To help them go mad they had rain, snow, frost, wind, and seas of mud. The trenches acted as drainage ditches for the land and even duckboards could not cope with the amounts of water that gathered in them. They soon became fouled by sewage, rotting vegetation and even flesh. The trenches were unhealthy. Never warm and seldom dry, the men suffered woefully from trench foot – a painful swelling of water-sodden flesh that would rot if not attended.

The mud was an awful problem. It was so deep and so liquid that men sometimes drowned in it. Guns got bogged down in it and the men spent days on end digging transports and themselves out of it. At times, they laid railway track and pushed flatcars along it to keep supplies moving forward, and at others they fitted guns with the special Boydell footed-wheel attachments to try to stop them sinking into the mud. It was a never-ending battle against the thick slime.

Days spent in the trenches were supposedly limited but duties varied according to military need and sometimes men spent weeks rather than days in the lines. When not in the line they were stationed in camps based around towns within 20 miles of the front. Here they could relax and 'enjoy themselves' or, rather, return to the boredom of camp life with only cheap wine, imported beer and their own company and that of the regimental chaplain for solace. Passes were issued allowing the men to sample the night-life of small French or Belgian towns, but one suspects that this was not exactly exciting.

The soldiers of the First World War reaffirmed what the fighting men of every age had learnt – that war was a percentage mixture of boredom and abject terror.

THEIR WEAPONS

The soldiers who fought in France and Belgium between 1914 and 1918 were faced with a technological revolution, the full implications of which were often beyond the grasp of their commanders. They began the war with rapid-fire weapons but with no real understanding of their power or effect upon tactics. The type of weapons changed and the type of explosive propellant changed; the ranges grew longer and the weight of shells grew heavier; but the drill books were not generally rewritten and the experiences of the men seldom listened to. The potential of developments of war in the air and tank combat were not seen, and what today might

---

LIFE IN THE TRENCHES

All regiments differed, but this was a typical routine:

- 'Stand-to', just before dawn and dusk, when everyone mounted the 'fire step' as this was the most obvious time for an enemy attack

- Unofficial truce while both sides ate breakfast

- Rifle inspection followed by fatigue parties, to repair trenches, and other work

- Lunch at noon

- More fatigues

- Dinner at 6 p.m.

- Dusk 'stand-to' for about an hour

- Officers' inspection. Following this, troops were divided into groups and either sent down the communication trenches to fetch rations from the quartermaster, or out on patrol, or to catch a little sleep. There was rarely a time when the vast majority of the soldiers were not awake and working. Fatigue was one of the greatest problems at the Front. It was not unknown for sentries to fall asleep while pacing out their beat in the trenches, and they were sometimes found hundreds of yards from their own regiment

- Machine-gunners were among the few groups of soldiers who were spared fatigues. Others included stretcher bearers and snipers

- Officers rarely had to undertake heavy work but lack of sleep was a real problem. A mass of paperwork occupied any hours that were not taken up with patrols, inspecting the men or organising sentries and fatigue parties

When not in the front line, soldiers were stationed in camps based around towns within 20 miles of the front

appear obvious was strange and indeed alien. As the fighting men and their senior officers came to terms with the changes, so the new quickly became obsolete as another innovation arrived, bringing faster and more deadly tools of the soldier's trade. The First World War became an arms race and the men guinea pigs to arm with something bigger and faster. It was a feeling that embraced all materials of the war and all aspects of the fighting.

Rifles: The introduction of a much more efficient and powerful propellant such as cordite spelt the end for the Metford system of rifling. Cordite burnt at a much higher temperature and caused a greater degree

Model	Calibre	Weight (lb/oz)	Magazine Capacity	Muz. Velocity (ft per sec)	Effective Range (yd)
Lee Enfield Mk III 1907	.303	8 lb 10 oz	10	2,060	600
Enfield Pattern 14 1916	.303	8 lb 11 oz	5	2,785	600
Lebel Mle 1893	8 mm		8		
Mauser Gewehr 1898	7.92		5		
Mannlicher Model 1895	8 mm		5		
US Model 1903	.3		5		

of barrel and breech erosion. This, combined with the new cupro-nickel jacket surrounding the lead bullet, reduced the 'life' of the Lee-Metford rifle to about 4,000 rounds. The Royal Small Arms factory at Enfield developed a different system and evolved a different barrel to produce the Lee Enfield Mk I 1895 model. It fired the .303 brass-case cartridge, was 49½ in long and was sighted up to 2,800 yd. The Boer War produced a demand for shorter pattern rifles that were easier to handle, lighter to carry and less of an encumbrance to use when fighting prone. Designers listened to veterans and the Short, Magazine, Lee Enfield Mk I, known as the SMLE, was introduced in 1902. It was nearly 1 lb lighter, 5 in shorter with a stock that reached to the muzzle, and the breech incorporated charger guides. Loading was easier too, as 2 clips of 5 cartridges could be inserted instead of loading each round singly. Conversions were named the Mk II but further improvements, including a U backsight, a foresight protected by a blade and wings, and better charger guides, resulted in the Mk III of 1907. By 1912, it was the standard weapon for the British Infantry, whose marksmen, trained as snipers, received the even newer Pattern 14 rifle. It was extremely accurate, especially when fitted with telescopic sights. During the early months of the war, the accuracy and rapidity of fire possible in the hands of trained regulars made the Germans believe they were facing machine-guns. The Canadians entered the war with a much inferior weapon, the Ross Rifle. It was different in design of both bolt and magazine from the Lee Enfield and followed the Mauser tradition of the magazine being in the stock, locked in place by the trigger guard.

Towards the end of the war, another type of rifle came into use. It used some of the force from the explosion of the cartridge to re-cock the striker and feed the breech with the next round. It thus became self-loading and did away with manual lever and bold action re-cocking systems. Some fired one round per squeeze of the trigger but others, at the turn of a switch, could fire bursts. The self-loading rifle was the prototype for the Second World War assault rifle.

Automatic revolvers: The double action revolver produced the first self-loading pistol by employing the force of the explosion, or the excess gases produced, to eject the spent case and insert the next round. George Luger modified the Borchardt recoil-operated pistol, producing a gun in 1898 with a magazine or clip of eight cartridges inserted in the hand-grip set upon a spring. The recoil of the shot operated a pair of toggle-like arms at the rear of the barrel, which ejected the case and opened the breech for the spring to push home the next cartridge. It was one of the first so-called automatic pistols. Luger produced a range of designs employing this system, including one which had a shoulder stock. By 1896 the Mauser had arrived with its 10-shot magazine set in front of the trigger guard; this was the gun that probably saved young

Model	Calibre (mm)	Magazine Capacity
Mondragon		
Modelo 1908	7	8
RSC Modele 1917	8	

Winston Churchill from certain death at the hands of the Mahdists. Because of a polo shoulder injury, he luckily charged with the 17th Lancers with his pistol rather than an officer's sword and emptied all ten rounds fighting his way out of the donga at Omdurman. By 1897, both Browning and Colt were manufacturing similar weapons. In 1901 the Webley Fosberry appeared; after a primary manual cock it too used expanding gas to revolve the cylinder and re-cock the action automatically. To reload, it broke in the centre, giving easy access to the cylinder, and had a spring-arm ejection system. The Webley had a supposed rate of fire of 12 shots in 20 seconds, making it a favourite of the British forces in the trenches and, indeed, it was still carried during the Second World War. Initially only issued to officers, revolvers were useful in the hand-to-hand combat of trench fighting and so they were 'acquired' by many of lesser rank. Ammunition for a captured or even non-issued gun was hard to come by, so robbing the dead became a common occurrence as the men scrabbled about to get the bullets for their 'life-saver'.

Mauser c/96 'Broomhandle' semi-automatic 7.63 or 9 mm. This model, with shoulder stock/holster, dates from c. 1915. Also shown is a First World War Iron Cross, 2nd class, an infantry belt and a 1916 Stahlhelm. (Painting by Chris Collingwood; see Useful Addresses)

Model	Calibre	Weight (lb/oz)	Magazine	Muz. Velocity (ft per sec)	Effective Range (yd)
Webley Mk VI 1915	.455	2 lb 4 oz	6 cyl	655	15
Lebel Modele 1892	8 mm		6 cyl		
Nagant Model 1895	7.62		7 cyl		
Modello 1889B	10.35		6 cyl		
Colt Navy Service 1917	.45		6 cyl		
Borchardt 1893	7.63				
Browning Modele 1900	7.65				
Mauser 1916	9 mm				

Machine-guns: The importance of rapid-fire multi-shot guns had shown itself in the American Civil War and the Pony Wars but had been ignored by the European military. Only the German Army had studied the effect of machine-guns (in the Anglo-Boer (1899–1902) and the Russo-Japanese Wars of 1904–05) and fully understood the lessons they taught. They equipped their men with sufficient Maxims by 1914 to gain a defensive advantage in the early stages of the war. They could push forward but the Allies could not push them back. As the First World War gathered momentum, machine-guns more and more became key weapons on the front and tactics changed to make full use of their fast rate and concentration of fire. Infantry advances had to be supported so lighter, more portable versions of the heavy tripod varieties were designed. The heavy machine-guns were used in static defensive positions, often firing on fixed lines, while the light machine-guns were carried into action and set up where necessary. The lighter weight also meant that they could be taken into the air, bolted to the new flying machines.

The Vickers gun of 1915 was an evolution of the Maxim. It had the same basic single barrel and belt feed idea but incorporated all the latest refinements. It had a water jacket, which kept it cool, and it was recoil- and gas-operated; each canvas belt now held 250 brass-cased .303 bullets. The first round had to be hand-cranked into position for firing, using the cocking lever. The recoil and the gases moved the breech block backwards, which ejected the spent case and fed the next cartridge into place. It weighed 30 lb and was usually mounted on a low tripod with a 360° arc of fire.

In action, the gun was often trained on a target and the tripod clamped in position, limiting the traverse. The gunner could adjust the line and elevation and change the cone of concentration within the designated target area. It was highly manoeuvrable, being manned by a section team of four men: two carried it (one had the barrel, the other the tripod), while the other two carried two ammunition boxes, each holding two full belts – that is eight complete belts with 2,000 rounds. (In India a team also had a mule capable of carrying both parts of the gun plus two belts, or a total of

The Vickers gun was highly manoeuvrable, being manned by a team of four men; two carried it (one held the barrel, the other the tripod); while the other carried the two ammunition boxes each holding full belts – that is, eight complete belts with 2,000 rounds

Attaching the Vickers machine-gun to the tripod

The gun was water cooled by means of a metal jacket around the barrel. A pipe was attached to this jacket . . .

ten belts.) It had a cyclic rate of fire of 500 rounds per minute but judicious use could make a belt last much longer than 30 seconds. In a fixed defensive position, when rapidly pouring fire into an advancing formation was the key to stemming an attack successfully, the gunner would have an ample supply of ammunition boxes in a dugout ready-magazine.

. . . and the other end of the pipe was placed in a water container

Each canvas belt of .303 brass-cased bullets held twenty-five rounds

The Lewis gun of 1915 was also gas-operated and, although it could be described as more of an automatic rifle than a machine-gun, it was brought into the British Army in significant numbers in 1915 to compensate for the enormous losses of skilled marksmen the BEF had sustained over the first few months of the war. It too was single-barrelled but air-cooled and had to

The Lewis gun of 1915 was gas-operated and, although more of an automatic rifle, it was brought into the British Army in significant numbers to compensate for the enormous losses of skilled marksmen

be fired in bursts of no more than thirty rounds if overheating troubles were to be avoided. It also fired the now standard .303 cartridges but they were fed into the breech via flat drum-shaped magazines that were fitted above the barrel and held only forty-seven rounds apiece. The need to change the drum frequently made it difficult to use, especially in the air in a single seater, where one hand at least was needed to fly the aeroplane. However, with proper crewing it could produce a cyclic rate of 550 rounds per minute and it weighed just under the Maxim at 26 lb, including bipod. It was sighted to 1,900 yd – over a mile.

Modification was the name of the game and, in 1914, Hotchkiss redesigned its 1896 model and introduced a gas-operated, air-cooled heavy machine-gun that was fed strips of cartridges. Browning's 1895 gas-operated model was revamped several times, including a shift to a recoil-operated one in 1901 and water cooling in 1917. Several nations manufactured their own version of the Maxim but the French used the recoil-operated Chauchat from 1915. As time went on so two classes of machine-gun evolved, light and heavy. One was for supporting attacks and was carried forward in action and used to inflict wounds at close range, while the other was employed in defence where stopping power at some distance was desired.

Model	Calibre	Weight (lb/oz)	Rate of Fire (rpm)	Operation	Feed	Cooling
LMGs:						
Lewis 1915	.303	26 lb	550	Gas	Drum Mag.	Air
Madsen 1903	8 mm	20 lb	450	Recoil	Curved Mag.	Air
Hotchkiss (British) 1916	.303	27 lb	500	Gas	Strip/Belt	Air
Maxim (German) 1908	7.92	27 lb	500	Recoil	Belt	Water
Chauchat 1914	8 mm	20 lb	250	Recoil	1/2 Dish Mag.	Air
HMGs:						
Browning-Colt 1914	.30	101 lb	450	Gas	Belt	Air
Hotchkiss (French) 1914	8 mm	88 lb	600	Gas	Strip	Air
Maxim (Russian)	7.62	152 lb 8 oz	600	Recoil	Belt	Water
Maxim (German) 1914	7.92	70 lb 8 oz	450	Recoil	Belt	Water
Schwarlose 1912	8 mm	44 lb	400	Blowback	Belt	Water
Fiat-Revelli 1914	6.5	37 lb 8 oz	500	Delay Blowback	Clip	Water
Vickers 1915	.303	30 lb	500	Recoil/Gas	Belt	Water

By 1918, the German Army had developed another type of machine-gun; this one was designed for one man to carry and used in place of the rifle. The Bergmann MP 18 was one of the first sub-machine-guns. It fired a 9 mm round and had a rate of 400 rpm, which would have made it a devastating weapon if it could have been produced in numbers and issued before the general collapse of the will to fight.

Artillery: The traditional field gun was still very much in demand, although bigger and better versions were constantly sought. The Boer War had taught the European gunners that they were vulnerable to small arms fire and so a shield was introduced to cover them while they fired the piece. Most shields folded down and had sighting holes cut through them,. They could stop a bullet but they did not have a wide protecting arc, being more beneficial to morale than able to save lives.

The British took a collection of 18- and 13-pdrs, plus 4.5 and 6 in howitzers to France in 1914. Along with them went one 9.2 siege howitzer and some ex-Boer War 4.7 guns and 5 in howitzers. It was efficient but elderly equipment. The artillery strength of the BEF in France at the end of 1914 was recorded as 6 batteries of 13-pdrs, 54 of 18-pdrs, 18 of 4.5 in howitzers and 9 of various heavy guns including the 4.7s, 5s and 6s.

The Home Defence force had 7 batteries of obsolete 15-pdrs and 12 in the Reserve. In total, the army had about 650 guns. In a very short time, this was to prove extremely inadequate in number and calibre. In Germany and Britain, both the great gun foundry of Krupps and the Woolwich Arsenal stepped up production, while negotiations with American manufacturers got underway. The whole world of the arms dealers got a massive financial injection in the race for guns. German and French artillery also varied in quality and quantity, and grew progressively heavier and bigger as the war went on. Each nation employed what had previously been classed as siege or coastal artillery to throw shells at their enemies as the race to produce bigger explosions and deal out more death grew ever more intense.

Model	Calibre	Shell Weight (lb/oz)	Charge Weight (lb/oz)	Gun Weight (tons)	Max. Range (yd)
British 12-pdr BL	3.0	12 lb 8 oz	12 oz	0.75	6,000
13-pdr QF	3.0	12 lb 8 oz	1 lb 4 oz	0.95	5,900
18-pdr QF	3.3	18 lb 8 oz	1 lb 7 oz	1.25	6,525
German 77 m QF	3.03	15 lb			9,200
French 75 m					
4.5 in QF How.	4.5	35 lb	1 lb	1.35	7,300
6 in Howitzer	6.0	100 lb			9,500
German 16.5 Howitzer	42 cm	205 lb			
British 12 in Howitzer	30.5 cm	750 lb		38	14,350
German Paris Gun	23.2 cm				75 miles
French Railroad Howitzer	40 cm	1,984 lb		unknown	17,500

The ammunition allowance and supply system was also inadequate for the artillery duels. In 1914 each British gun was technically allocated eight shells per day, but by 1915 they were required to be firing in the region of 100 every day and more in preparation for an attack. This put a tremendous strain upon supply, manufacture and cost. Recent research has investigated the measures taken by the high command to limit the spending and their correspondence with government officials and manufacturers is earning the intriguing title of the Great Shell Scandal.

Trench mortars: Early experiments with modern mortars were dangerous for the crews and the men did not like them. Designed to throw a series of small bombs at high trajectory angles so that they fell into the enemy's trenches, the system remained muzzle-loading and each bomb had an impact ignition charge to enable drop-firing. This proved to be unreliable and erratic. Dropping a bomb down a tube without any assurance of when it would fire was a risky business. To counter this, the German Minenwerfer was rifled and its bombs were fitted with a pre-engraved copper driving band that matched up with the rifling in the bore, making drop-loading impossible and demanding a separate firing mechanism. These were more popular as they gave the loader chance to step clear of the muzzle before the bomb went off.

Other weapons: Small night-time raids on enemy trenches, launched to capture a prisoner or reinforce a spying mission, required quiet stealth weapons for hand-to-hand combat in confined spaces, and a whole range of trench-knives was produced. Some were sophisticated, with stiletto or fold-away blades, while others were resharpened broken bayonets or double-edged kitchen utensils, saw blades or even razor-sharp knitting needles.

The Mk I hand grenade could prove as dangerous to the thrower as to the intended victim

Fighting in the trenches if a full assault got home was also frantic and vicious with men using their bayonets and a wealth of improvised weaponry. One innovation was the hand grenade. Ignored for many years, the hand-thrown bomb came back into its own because of the short sections of trenches to be cleared, their zigzag construction that afforded protection to the thrower, and the need to lob an explosive into works, over parapets and down into dugouts. The Mk I was a long-handled design with an impact (mining) detonator and it proved dangerous to those who threw it. It was the perfection of the cast-iron oval Mills Bomb, with its lever, pin and 5-second delayed fuse action that led to the general issue of grenades, which remained popular in British service until the 1960s.

Above, left: The bayonet socketed onto the rifle might have been the dream weapon of the officers and senior NCOs but its only real military use was as a short stabbing and slashing sword; other than that its primary functions were to open ration tins and split firewood for cooking; right: Soldiers chose their own trench weapons; this is a knuckle-duster headed knife

The bayonet socketed onto the rifle might have been the dream weapon of the officers and senior NCOs but its only real military use was as a short stabbing and slashing sword; other than that its primary functions were to open ration tins and split firewood for cooking.

The men chose their own trench weapons and, once again, many sought inspiration from medieval warfare, producing falchions, flails, nail-headed clubs, hammers, maces and axes with the added refinements of built-in knuckle-dusters, marlin spikes and gloves wrapped in barbed wire. The pretension to an age of elegance with rules of engagement was definitely over.

Armoured vehicles: The idea of fighting from a vehicle was not new – the Egyptians had used chariots, war wagons had been used by the Hussites, and da Vinci had designed several mobile war machines in the fifteenth century – but the petrol engine and the motor car had made it a much better proposition. Early in the war, armour was fixed to cars, and most nations used them for scouting and raiding purposes. They were fast but they could not deliver much punch. The idea of the tank was slow in developing, and its supporters had to fight a long battle with both the die-hards of the military and the bureaucrats of governments. They were sold the idea of the tank as a machine-gun destroyer, something to break the trench deadlock and protect an attack from the deadly rapid fire.

A new weapon was forged; a lozenge-shaped, steel container similar to a water tank was evolved as this was best suited to an enveloping caterpillar tracking system and to deflecting bullets. It could span trenches, drive over or through the wire, and spray machine-gun bullets of its own while going forward – later models were to have 6-pdr guns as well as machine-guns. The first tanks went into action on 15 September 1916 and performed adequately, although not brilliantly. Secrecy and choice of ground posed too many problems. However, they did break through the German lines and caused significant morale problems. Given the right ground, these new weapons were a great advantage and proved so on many occasions. They were used in tight cooperation with infantry and carried firepower forward, breaking down obstacles and over-running trenches, while offering protection to the assault troops themselves. However, they were never properly supported, especially at Cambrai, and the breaks in the line they caused were not exploited by reserve squadrons; thus, the potential of the tank was not realised. It was left to those upon whom the tanks first advanced in the First World War to understand their power and to forge the panzer units destined to create a new form of warfare and to roll over Europe.

Most of the early tanks had a fairly standard 12 mm thick steel plate armour, but by 1918 designers were incorporating 14 mm, and by the time the Mk 8 came out in 1919 it was up to 16 mm, while the Rolls Royce armoured car remained at the lighter 9 mm throughout its service.

Model	Weight (tons)	Crew	Road Speed (mph)	Operating range (miles)	Armament
Rolls Royce AC 1914	3.5	3	45	180	1×MG
Mk 1 Male 1916	28	8	3.5	24	2×6-pdrs 4×MGs
Mk 5 Male 1918	29	8	4.5	35	2×6-pdrs 4×MGs
Medium A Whippet 1918	14	4	8	40	4×MGs
Medium C Hornet	19.5	4	8	75	4×MGs

THEIR FIGHTING

Armies were still organised in very much the same way as they had been throughout the nineteenth century, except that now regiments had far more battalions than one in the field and one in reserve at the depot. Some regiments had up to twenty battalions recruited from all over the country and held together only by name and number. The Pals Battalions gradually coalesced into fewer and fewer units, until a single regiment could no longer be formed from their numbers, at which point they were sometimes amalgamated with other reduced units from a similar region or of a similar make-up. Small specialist units were formed, usually to man, crew or serve a new type of weapon. If successful, they were enlarged and funded and thus eventually the Royal Air Force and the Royal Tank Regiment came into being. If they were failures, then they were disbanded or allowed to 'melt' until amalgamation.

One of the major points that emerged from study of the Russo-Japanese War was that artillery and infantry had to cooperate again. Napoleonic gunners had fought alongside their infantry but, with the dramatic increase in gun range, the artillery had been placed further and further in the rear, often in concealed positions. To enable the guns to support the infantry, 'Forward Observing Officers' were sent to the infantry and given orders to report back to senior gunners who would decide what action to take based upon the situation as it had been described; under no circumstances was the power of decision to be handed over to the infantry. There was little or no direct communication between the two arms although they were ordered to act in concert together. The idea, as far as the artillery high command was concerned, was to throw in a preparatory barrage, of ever-increasing proportions, until it was time to let the infantry do their bit.

As this was a new kind of barrage warfare, with massed guns on a scale that Napoleon could only have dreamt of and rapid-firing small arms that would have gratified Marlborough's determination to produce continuous fire, the men on both sides dug trenches to protect themselves from the raking fire of the rifles, machine-guns and the artillery. As each attack became bogged down against a network of trenches so armies would swing this way or that in an attempt to outmanoeuvre each other, only to meet another stretch of frenetically entrenched defences. In a few months, more than 400 miles of trenches swept in a long line across northern France, from Switzerland to the sea. As the German advance petered out against such works, they too dug in more deeply. If they could not push foward, then they would ensure that Allies would not drive them back. The positions had to be held to prevent the line being broken, so men settled down to a stalemate of trench warfare.

Concentration of rifle fire on specific points to suppress enemy fire in preparation for a bayonet charge (the tactics of the Boer War) still held good for the early months, but the increased numbers of machine-guns being deployed in the lines made it a heavy casualty business, even when open order was allowed. It was really the machine-gun that caused the dramatic change in tactics by rendering massed infantry attacks both costly and futile. It was largely responsible for the stalemate of the trenches. Trench systems were complicated, a warren of parallels and communication trenches, zigzags and bunkers, dugouts and machine-gun nests, with deeply dug shelters in which to take refuge during artillery bombardment.

Attacking infantry were assembled in the front trenches shortly before 'zero hour', and, at the appointed time, the officers blew whistles and fired flares to signal a general advance. The belief was that by saturating the front with men an attack could be pressed home. As the first wave went across No Man's Land, the second wave assembled and was sent over the top minutes later, to be followed by the third wave. It was the old Napoleonic cavalry tactics applied to infantry. The first unit is the assault force, which spends itself in disrupting the enemy; the second is the support, which widens any gap in the line; and the third is the reserve, meant to break through and consolidate the gained advantage. But enemy entanglements of barbed wire slowed down the advance, reduced the charge to a tentative yet desperate hunt through a maze, and the machine-guns did the rest. The first and second waves were usually cut down in the few hundred yards of barren and cratered earth between the lines, while very few of the third ever reached the enemy. For a few years, some of the old-fashioned generals even clung doggedly to the notion of the cavalry charge sweeping through the gap smashed by the infantry and fanning out either side to wreak havoc among the enemy's unprotected rear lines.

Suppression of enemy fire was still fixed firmly in the minds of the generals and they believed the answer lay in heavy artillery bombardment, which would pulverise the emplacements, flatten the wire and kill hundreds of the defenders. Several hours of continuous heavy shelling preceded attacks in which men often went mad with the noise and with fear but, after it stopped, they crawled out of the deep shelters dragging their machine-guns with them to mow down the infantry as it tried yet again to get across those few hundred yards of instant death.

Such was the tactical inflexibility that almost every attack resulted in thousands of casualties. Both sides committed the same heinous errors of military judgement and both sides lost generations of young men to the machine-guns. The major fault lay in the lack of communications. Radio was in its infancy and too unreliable. Field telephones were tried, with men paying out long lines of wire as they advanced, but these wires were easily cut. Runners were frequently shot, and carrier pigeons and dogs were just too limited in flexibility.

When an attack went in, the commanders lost all control. Artillery and infantry were coordinated by wrist-watch and, should a single machine-gun delay an attack from being at a specific point, even by a few minutes, men would fall prey to their own guns. There was no way of telling when an attack was failing and stopping the reinforcement of a disaster. Similarly, there was no way to call in reserves to exploit an unexpected gain. Likewise, reconnaissance was scant, and the army distrusted the airmen who risked their lives to provide information about enemy troop dispositions and movements. The fighting men had to do it by the book and according to an HQ plan, despite the 'book' being written twenty years before and the plan being drawn up without decent intelligence and without any contingencies made for changing situations. How to solve these problems was not really considered by either side, as they sought a war-winning weapon to end the trench stalemate.

Breaking the deadlock became a key debate. At one time mines were thought to be the solution, and today huge craters mark sites in Belgium and northern France where they were detonated. At another stage, short-range and high trajectory mortars were favoured, and the Trench Mortar Service was put together – unofficially it was dubbed 'The Suicide Club'. Hand grenades too were once thought of as war-winning weapons, and then came poison gas in its several distasteful forms. But there persisted the notion that the real war-winning weapon was eventually going to be the cavalry, if ever they got the opportunity.

The cavalry were still employed as shock weapons at the beginning of the war, with the French Cuirassiers even going into action in plumed helmets and breastplates. While this 'game' was played by the German Uhlans all went well, but when either side ran into infantry, their efforts ended in carnage. The switch to mounted infantry fared little better, for they were shot down or blown apart as they rode to a position. Cavalry had reached its final phases of usefulness on the battlefield. The horse had had its day, but the senior officers still kept regiments of cavalry stationed behind any attack, ready gloriously to exploit any advantage won by the infantry. Unfortunately, they fell victim to overshots by enemy artillery and if their position was detected by enemy reconnaissance it would betray to them the exact point where the major pressure was going to fall.

A couple of times they did charge. Private Clarke of the Suffolks recalled seeing three Indian cavalry regiments thread their way through the wire, deploy in front of his section of the trenches and charge over him as his lay in a shell hole. He counted eleven men return still mounted.

The men were usually shot through the legs but the horses suffered awfully, especially from unflattened barbed wire. Those wounded terribly were shot by their riders, others were brought back and shipped home. So fixed was the idea that cavalry could be the war-winning factor, that healing horses was a prime concern. Swindon, in the south of England, was a centre for the recuperation of horses wounded at the front and locals tell of the horrendous gaping wounds that were stitched up by a team of vets and farm hands, working in relays, to get them patched up and back into service.

But the horse was finished as a battlefield factor. The scouting and reconnaissance roles were shifted to the air and the brave pilots who threw themselves around the skies in flimsy canvas and wood contraptions. These pilots could fly over the enemy lines and make notes on troop movements, concentrations and strength of defences. Freely acquired information was soon countered by the men using their own revolvers, rifles and even shotguns in the air. The Flying Corps found themselves the day-to-day heroes of aerial duels and, as skirmishes between these aircraft increased, the make-do weaponry carried by the pilots and observers gave way to properly fitted machine-guns with timed mechanisms, synchronised with the engine, to enable them to shoot through the rotating propeller. They

also dropped projectiles from the aeroplanes, ranging from weighty darts to hand-held, impact-fused bombs. Bombing from the air became a reality and the battlefield had its first taste of combat air support. By the formation of the RAF, the cavalry had lost its strategic strike role as well as its job as the eyes and ears of the army.

The cavalry also lost its shock effect role, this time to the tank. The tank was a metal monster on caterpillar tracks that could roll across the craters in No Man's Land and penetrate the enemy line without being hampered by the wire or machine-gun fire. It was a war-winning weapon, for all its early imperfections and disasters. Infantry following tanks found protection and a cleared pathway. Combined arms operations speeded up the war and broke the stalemate, albeit in a piecemeal fashion. In March 1918 the Germans employed a new advance technique. Armed with smaller, light machine-guns, small parties rushed forward in short bursts under covering fire from each other. This was successful and was quickly copied by the Allies. It was to set the pattern for peacetime training and the low level tactics of the Second World War.

Although the machine-gun caused the trench situation, if the First World War was to belong to one weapon it must be reckoned as the war of the artillery. After the initial stalemate in the trenches and the artillery attempts to flatten the wire and cave in the forward lines for an assault that never really went home, the 'final solution' came in a consuming faith in big guns. Bigger and bigger artillery pieces were deployed, hurling bigger and bigger explosive charges further and further. At the beginning of the war, a single battery of field artillery required 168 horses to move it; by the end of 1917, tractors and other vehicles had been utilised. The heaviest pieces had even been mounted on railway flatcars, towed to within 20 miles of the target and then uncoupled to fire, the recoil being channelled by the track and the engine recoupled to pull it back into position.

The sheer scale of artillery bombardment had never been seen before. Each gun consumed hundreds of shells every day. Supply became an intense problem, and increased demand on manufacturing threw up trade union problems as civilian workers refused to work nights and rejected moves to import unskilled night-shift labour. Some modern historians have argued that the First World War could have been much shorter if trade unions had been abolished in time of war, while others, of a different political persuasion, argue that putting a country's defence into private hands helped to prolong the war through a deliberate international agreement between arms manufacturers to maximise profits. Whatever the reasoning, to the British civilians in the factories the war, if only just across the Channel, was still a distant thing and the army, dependent upon private commercial companies as contractors, was powerless to do anything about it.

The nature of the war demanded heavier pieces. Orders went through for heavier howitzers to bombard the entrenched positions and for bigger

THE FIRST WORLD WAR

shells with greater explosive power to send shockwaves down through the earth and collapse tunnels and dugouts, shatter copulas and fracture concrete fortifications. The army also called for long-range guns, which could reach far behind the enemy lines to explode fuel and ammunition dumps, smash railways and roads and even pound known enemy headquarters.

At the start of the war, the main anti-personnel projectile was the shrapnell shell. Detonated by a time fuse, it sprayed a wide arc of bullets over an area of ground as it descended. This was improved by adding an impact detonator to make up for any fault in the timing system. Gradually, the shrapnell shell was superseded by the high explosive shell, which employed blast and fragmentation. It began with a delayed impact fuse but the mud sometimes absorbed the shock of landing and shells did not explode, so they were fitted with time or proximity fuses to produce the airburst effect that could detonate directly above a trench and cause havoc in its downblast.

The third type of common projectile was the chemical shell, which often delivered lethal gas. The casing was filled with a chemical liquid that, when scattered by a small impact charge and exposed to air, created a poisonous fog which dissolved the lungs and blinded anyone coming into contact with it. Between them, shockwave HE, shrapnel, anti-personnel HE and chemical shells took the war to the enemy no matter how he dug in, as gunners pounded the battlefield from positions a couple of miles away.

By 1916, the supply of heavy guns started to increase and they were beginning to become the masters of the battlefield, and the men mere tolerated inhabitants. The heavy guns now did the killing, not the machine-guns, and it was the heavy guns too that shattered the nerves of those who had to endure their constant shelling. The First World War evolved into an artillery duel. The wire and the machine-gun held the enemy still, pinning him down on a particular spot; the mud and the long-range gunnery prevented relief or reinforcement; and the short-range, heavy artillery systematically blasted him to pieces or pounded his brain to jelly. The age of attrition warfare had arrived in deadly earnest.

Above: Stand-to – at dawn and dusk. The entire line would stand on the fire step (a ledge allowing the soldier to aim his rifle above the parapet). These were the most likely times for an enemy attack

Opposite, above: After dawn stand-to, a brief pause for breakfast before resuming the daily round of hard work and staying alive; below: sentry duty was necessary and unpleasant. The sentry would either have a 'beat' to patrol or remain stationary. It has been recorded that some sentries, while on night guard, were required to stand with their head and shoulders above the trench parapet to maintain a greater degree of vigilance

After two or three hours of duty the sentry would have the same period for sleep and then be available for fatigues

Time to wash and shave was very limited, if
available at all. The insanitary conditions in the
trenches led to infestations of lice, fleas and rats

Few comforts existed, perhaps a brew-up of tea on a small stove

Food was often eaten straight from a can, or immersed in boiling water for a few minutes

The Greatcoat was a substantial piece of clothing, weighing 7 lb. However, in the frequent Flanders rain, the coat would absorb 20 lb of water. This, plus adhering mud, could weigh up to 34 lb, and added unbearably to the average weight of 60 lb of equipment carried

Minimum equipment

Greatcoat	Latherbrush	Pay book
Mess tin	Comb	Bootlaces
Towel	Toothbrush	150 rounds of ammunition
Housewife	Tin of Grease	Rifle and bayonet
Shirt	Knife, fork, spoon	Rifle cover
Holdall	Field dressing	Entrenching tool
Socks (3 pairs)	Gas mask	Bottle of oil
Razor and comb	Spine protector	Water bottle
Soap	Cap comforter	

Each night fresh supplies were brought up to the front line, including mail and rations. It was a hazardous journey through stinking communication trenches, often thigh- high in mud, amid shells exploding with thunderous regularity

Letters from home. Over 12 million letters were
sent out to the front each week. It took no more
than two or three days for them to arrive

Duckboards were placed in the trenches in an effort to combat the water and mud, often without success

An ever-present threat was death from a sniper's bullet. The snipers themselves were prime targets and suffered a heavy toll

'Caught a Blighty'. Artillery shells rained metal fragments onto the trenches causing widespread injury and death. An injury severe enough to return the soldier home was termed a 'Blighty', 'Blighty' being the slang for Great Britain. 'Catching a Blighty' was the only chance some soldiers had of home leave

Gas alert. Gas was first used at the second battle of Ypres in 1915. This most obnoxious of weapons was released either by artillery shell or from cylinders. It caused blindness and severe lung damage. Mustard gas was one of the worst – blistering the skin, causing painful eyes, vomiting and nausea as well as stripping the lungs. The gas smelled 'sweet as a bon-bon'. It took twelve hours for the effects to become apparent and then subjected its victims to weeks of extreme agony before death

Humour is often the only refuge for a fighting man under pressure, and many dealt with the horrors in this way

Front line company headquarters dug-out. An
officer receives the order to attack the enemy
trenches the next morning; the order would then be
relayed to the NCOs. Communications were
unreliable whether by land line (prone to being cut
by artillery shells) or, less often, by carrier pigeon,
dogs or both

The word spreads. To some, it is the last straw, adding to the agony of shell shock and extreme physical and mental discomfort. Others accept the news quietly, their main fear being that of showing fear

Dusk stand-to

Each man is isolated by his own thoughts as the time approaches; the pulse thumping in his ears, his mouth dry, the tot of rum hardly noticed

As dawn breaks, the soldiers prepare for the assault – their own big guns fall silent after pounding the German lines

Over the top!

No longer in the relative safety of the trenches, the soldiers are fully exposed to a vicious hail of lead. Wave after wave of men went 'over the top'; thousands upon thousands did not return

The machine-gunners keep the gun low; they are the first target for the enemy

THE SECOND WORLD WAR

THE SECOND WORLD WAR

After the First World War the nations with the dubious accolade of 'victors' declared the cost of peace too high and determined that they should never again get involved in anything approaching armed nations in conflict. A whole generation of young men had been lost, and preparing for another similar war was anathema. France attempted to seal herself from Germany, the cause of so much conflict since 1870, with a state of the art defensive barrier called the Maginot Line; a fortified trench and tunnel system. Britain applied the Ten Year Plan, deferring any rearmament plans for a decade, which were subsequently extended until 1933. However, those defeated during the First World War felt

the cost could have been bearable if the outcome had been different. The Treaty of Versailles had been humiliating for Germany and Austria, and indeed Italy felt that it had not enjoyed its fair share of the spoils of victory. There is plenty of evidence of collective feelings of grievance against the victors, who commercially exploited their hard-won eminence.

During the 1920s this enmity was manifested in the growth of nationalist and paramilitary political parties in nations beaten in the First World War. Hitler led one such group but an attempted coup of his was crushed by the army in 1923. In response, he not only wooed army leaders, but also created his own militia of 100,000 so-called stormtroopers, raised on the politics of xenophobia and swept to power in 1933. Although forbidden to rearm, Colonel (later General) Heinz Guderian held manoeuvres with illegally constructed prototype tanks and carried out tests on the new Schmeisser. Impressed, Hitler renounced the Treaty of Versailles, reintroduced conscription and ordered three panzer divisions and the rearming of thirty-six infantry divisions to be ready by 1937, while employing the political machinery of National Socialism to imbue Germany with a nostalgia for its militaristic past and to cultivate the culture of the warrior élite.

By 1938, rearmament with the latest technology had been achieved, coupled with the production of 3,850 aircraft and the creation of the Luftwaffe. Rearmament was a popular policy, delivering full employment and an upsurge in national pride. Riding the success, the Nazis marched into the demilitarised Rhineland, incorporated Austria and annexed Sudetenland. Pandering to the desire for revenge and lauded military achievements, they organised society on military lines, staged theatrical military rallies, fostered the romance of the uniform and used the media to inculcate a joy in having modern tanks, aircraft, ships and weaponry – in short, they laid the foundations for another nation in arms.

By 1939, confident it could defeat what it proclaimed as its 'decadent neighbours', with every man again a soldier and inspired by those who had been cheated of victory by the arrival of the Americans in 1918, Germany attacked Poland. On Day One the Polish Air Force of 935 aeroplanes was eliminated and in 5 weeks her 40 infantry divisions with no armour had been crushed by Germany's 52 infantry and 10 armoured divisions. It was the testing of Hitler's new strategic warfare, Blitzkrieg, designed to deliver a powerful and unstoppable lightning strike, coordinated by radio contact, which kept rolling forward until it had destroyed or demoralised the enemy.

Having been tested successfully, Blitzkrieg was directed at Holland, Belgium and then France in May 1940. In three days it bypassed the Maginot Line, drove deep into French territory and then struck westward for the coast. Beating all before them, the German panzers, with air cover,

PRISONERS OF WAR

Surrender, to a soldier, was a shameful but sometimes inevitable option to needless sacrifice. Prisoners of war posed great problems of what to do with them, because post-1800 the economics and nationalism of war had a great influence. Rather than exchange or ransom the officers and let the common soldiers go or turn their coats, they were all considered a potential threat, part of the war effort that had to be neutralised. Imprisonment was the usual solution. Napoleonic prisoners were usually herded into churches or barns, then marched to ports and shipped back to their captor's country where they were often put into civil prisons. In Britain, thousands of unlucky Frenchmen were sent to the hulks; rotting decommissioned warships moored in unhealthy backwaters where the men spent their days locked in the airless lower decks. However, such massive overcrowding of an already over-stretched system caused a moral outcry and building began of specially constructed prisons for enemy soldiers. Besides accommodation, large numbers of prisoners also posed provision and sanitation problems and solutions were not always satisfactory.

The infamous Confederate Andersonville was a stockade, with corner sentry towers, that surrounded a small shallow valley. A stream running through the camp provided drinking water at one end, washing in the middle and latrines before it ran out – in summer this far end was a foul swamp. Provisions were rationed as the South could not even supply its fighting forces. Union prisoners got whatever meagre and often rancid food the corrupt administration could buy cheaply. Andersonville was overcrowded and provided no shelter; the men improvised tents from coats, shirts, sacks and whatever, but these gave little protection from the southern sun or the winter cold. Discipline was harsh, and brutal punishments severe. Dysentery, exposure, malnutrition and murder emptied the camp for others.

The Geneva Convention (1864) set out a code of practice for the treatment of prisoners of war. They were still stockaded and overcrowded, but camps had to provide shelter, warmth and sufficient, if not pleasant, food. The film industry has realistically portrayed Allied prisoners living in purpose-built, wooden huts behind the double, tall, barbed-wire fences of the Stalags. German prisoners were held in similar camps in remote parts of England and Wales – usually peace-time training barracks with lines of brick and 'wriggly tin' Nissen huts with a wire fence. In hotter climates, tents were used and there are some remarkable pictures of one or two 'Tommies' guarding several thousand Italians sitting in the desert behind a single strand of smooth wire. Officers had a 'duty' to escape but many private soldiers saw the POW camp as a refuge. People shouted at them, herded them about, fed them poorly, bored them for long periods and terrified them for short ones but this was better than the inhumanity of the battlefield.

Apprehensive or resigned, German prisoners were just fortunate soldiers for whom the war was over. Only one man is thought to have escaped successfully from a British POW camp

cut off the French and British forces in the north-west forcing the evacuation of Dunkirk. This pocket of resistance collapsed on 4 June and by the 17th France sued for peace. Blitzkrieg worked superbly, taking everything without much loss in men or equipment. It had produced 'real time war'; it convinced sceptical officers that the stalemate of the trenches was a thing of the past; and it showed politicians that Germany could achieve its aims without committing its entire economy to war. Since the American Civil War and the Anglo-Boer War, senior academics in strategic studies had ascribed eventual victory to the side most able and willing to gear its industry to the war effort – the higher the proportion of Gross National Product (GNP) risked, the greater the chance of victory. Blitzkrieg offered to break this model, with the caveat that weapon research and materials for its own renewal were not skimped.

John Keegan noted that Hitler was obsessed with the technology of war, the primacy of the warrior class and the Clausewitzian notion that war was the continuation of politics. With the production of revolutionary weapons as the objective of the manufacturing base, the indoctrination of the people with the warrior ethos as the intention of social manipulation, and the integration of war and politics as an indivisible entity, European war achieved an unprecedented level of totality. Total war was a new idea to western culture and it embraced the then staggering idea of deliberate civilian targets.

In the past civilian populations had been massacred by enraged troops storming a city or castle. It was usually blamed on lack of military control (such as happened at Badajoz), part of the rules of war (as enforced at Drogheda), religious fanaticism (as ran riot at Constantinople), or the actions of a criminal or lunatic leader. Killing civilians was classed as an atrocity but total war rendered it an integral part of the political process with the aim of terrorising an enemy people into submission rather than fighting and defeating their army. Bomber aircraft provided the means. The Germans had tried it with the Zeppelins during the First World War, but those unstable, slow moving and highly inflammable airships were never the correct technology. Hitler and Goering set the problem, Heinkel and Dornier supplied the efficient solution.

Between September 1940 and May 1942, the Luftwaffe blitzed London, destroyed much of Coventry and flattened large areas of other British cities. But the Battle of Britain saw the RAF victorious and the Luftwaffe was eventually forced to concede that a long-term bomber offensive was likely to be costly in aircraft and crews, and ultimately ineffective. These bombing attacks upon the civilian population of Britain failed to trigger the mass panic hoped for by Goering, but had he mounted a heavier and more sustained offensive the outcome might have been very different.

However, the application of strategic bombing by the RAF and USAAF was a different story altogether. Both air forces existed as the executors of independent air strategies, not simply as adjuncts of their respective national armies, as was the Luftwaffe. When 'Bomber' Harris mounted the first of the RAF's 1,000-bomber raids against Germany in May 1942, the writing was on the wall for the future annihilation of Germany. With the USAAF, the combined strategic air offensive that followed resulted in huge civilian casualties and the wholesale devastation of German industry on a scale previously undreamed of. On the other side of the world, waves of USAAF bombers systematically blasted and burned to the ground sixty-three Japanese cities. The enormity of the loss of civilian life and property caused a dramatic drop in the will of the people to resist.

Another feature of total war was the encouragement of barbaric treatment of the enemy. When the attack on Britain ground to a halt, Nazi Germany shifted its attention, first to lightning campaigns, taking Yugoslavia and Greece, and then in June 1941 to Russia. They easily overran the Ukraine but the severity with which they treated the Russian population, civilian and captured soldiers – 3 million Soviet POWs died of maltreatment during 1941–2 – actually strengthened the will to resist rather than weakened it.

In 1942, when the USA entered the war, Hitler's overall strategy was already cracking. Germany still concentrated upon the production of the weapons of Blitzkrieg – panzers, dive bombers and infantry automatic weapons – even though it meant supremacy at sea had been checked because of shortages in submarine building, and lack of research to block the development of sonar. Germany's air supremacy had been lost through a number of factors, not least the meddling of Hitler in the Luftwaffe's strategic planning and the sheer scale of sustained Allied aircraft production, the latter combined with the introduction of long-range day and night fighters and their lead in radar technology.

Supremacy in the east had been lost to the Russian T-34s. The German industrial machine was being ground down. Because of the success of Blitzkrieg it had never been committed to full war production and the country had never fully geared up to allocating 100 per cent GNP to the war. When Germany lost access to the oil fields of North Africa, the T-34 denied it the oil fields of Russia, and its synthetic petrol-chemical works were being bombed night and day, the industrial infrastructure, never properly asked for its maximum, crumbled. First Germany and then Japan was swamped by 'the surge of US industry' and the size of the US wallet.

The loss of German supremacy at sea and in the air made D-Day feasible, and the invasion of Normandy put a German army trained and skilled in offence into a defensive war. In Russia the mood changed too. Instead of rapid striking movements it became a bitter war of attrition, similar to that of the First World War, and the Soviets had far greater resources of people and materials. Although a nation in arms, Germany could not fight American industry and wealth, let alone Soviet manpower and unlimited natural resources.

Hitler's supremacy at sea had been checked by 1942

Not all Germans were Nazis

Still placing faith in new technology, Hitler unleashed the V1 flying bombs and began testing the V2 in the belief that they would force the overthrow of the British Government by war-weary civilians. Rockets were to revolutionise warfare completely yet again in the post-war years, but in 1945 the entire project was just too little, too late, and the German will to resist crumpled as the combined might of the Allied industrial nations rolled over the Third Reich. The Second World War had witnessed the birth of modern Blitzkrieg and the advent of 'total war' but even these two innovations could not reverse the grip that science and technology had on the conflict between men in 'real time war' and 'industrial might'.

British paratrooper. Military service was compulsory for all males, married or single, between the ages of eighteen and fifty

THE MEN

Despite the success of the early BEF in France in 1914, the notion of a trained professional army was still an expensive option to many politicians, and between the wars the regular army readopted its traditional social role as a home for the unemployable or destitute. However, the British Army of the Second World War was to benefit from politicians noting the effect of compulsory national service during the First World War, and as the politics of the late 1930s began to indicate a shift towards war, conscription was put into operation in 1938.

The territorials formed the initial backbone of the call-up but soon service applied to all males, married or single, between the ages of 18 and 50, and they were divided into the Expeditionary and Home Defence Forces, with extra-sensitivity placed upon coping with air-defence and anti-bombing measures. Men came from all backgrounds and social groups and although the major public schools still supplied the officer training establishments, young men from the upper middle classes found themselves serving alongside their countrymen from the back-to-back terraces. Sections and platoons were mixtures of backgrounds jumbled together in the glorious equality of the Nissen hut. They underwent basic training often without weapons – you do not need a rifle to learn how to march properly. Arms and equipment were slow in production as the nation was not ready to mobilise when called to do so, but the BEF still went over to France to what many thought would be a return to the trenches, while the HDF built pill-boxes, and coastal and field fortifications.

The German offensive tactics gave no time for trenches, and the BEF was undertrained and – despite all the lessons of the First World War – still officered by a social élite out of touch with technology. The army was saved only by the amphibious evacuation of Dunkirk. Many political 'We Shall Return' speeches resulted in more men joining the army, and with worldwide conflict the need for men brought in by drafts on the conscription plan became even more evident. However, the time for civilians in arms was over. The massive conscript armies had to be trained and conditioned to their new lives in the forces. They were indoctrinated into the ways and methods of the army, albeit very slowly.

At this time, the British Army had put 4 divisions into France, and it had 6 infantry and 1 armoured division in the Middle East, 1 division and 1 brigade in India, 2 brigades in Malaya, and several other colonial garrisons. Although obviously too small, it could not be enlarged quickly because of under-investment in the weapons industry and lack of financial commitment from a divided City. Once war was finally seen as inevitable, and the reverses of the first months unpalatably obvious, a new commitment by the Government, the people, industrialists and the financiers became apparent. It was the men of the RAF who bought Britain time to reorganise its nucleus of regulars and its influx of new recruits. Men

WOMEN AT WAR

Women from all over Britain and from every class donned uniforms to work for the war effort. Even Queen Elizabeth, then Princess Elizabeth, forsook her finery for the khaki drab. They may not have been 'in the teeth', but women served as truck drivers, mechanics, armourers and in many other dirty and some dangerous trades – as motorcycle despatch riders they would deliver documents, maps, and messages if the radio went down. Not exactly 'Hell's Angels', but it could be a hellish job, especially going at top speed at night with no lights because of the blackout. For others, the war meant volunteering for civilian duties, as well as the constant watching and waiting for their loved ones to return.

were conscripted and had to be housed and trained as best the army could. Many went into barracks that had changed little from Victorian times but others had the benefits of the new mood.

Typical of this, the Minister for War, Hore-Belisha, oversaw the introduction of new style barracks. They were two- or three-storey brick or stone buildings, with two blocks, one behind the other, and connected at one end by a vertical running annex with a communal stairway, NCO quarters, flush toilets and washrooms. Each floor thus had two self-contained barracks with controlled access. They each had a boiler house, which meant central heating and running hot water in the ablutions, and there was often a fireplace for additional warmth. They even had electric light. Inside the barracks the beds still ranked down the walls and the men lived out of neatly stacked lockers. The floors of polished wood still had to shine like the angels in all their glory to please the RSM, and the Victorian attitude to drill, discipline and keeping the men on their toes still reigned supreme.

Two of these blocks would be linked by a central cross-building, single-storied and housing the dining-hall and cookhouse, creating an elongated H shape. Both sergeants and officers had separate messes, and there was a series of single-storied administration offices and storerooms neatly laid out nearby. Also to hand were corrugated tin garages for the regimental vehicles and guns and usually a large hangar-type building for indoor training purposes. Married quarters too were in the vicinity, officers one side of the camp, ORs the other, along with medical and dental centres and general barracks services including the garrison church, shops and cinema.

The buildings were set amid spacious lawns, where weeds did not dare to grow, and everywhere was linked by sweeping curved roads and right-angled concrete paths marked by white-painted stones. These barracks of the late '30s, with their names recalling famous victories, were the most comfortable the British soldier had ever had and, indeed, are still better in quality and finish than much of the hastily thrown-up service accommodation of the '60s, although today they have been modernised to include well-furnished dormitories or partitioned rooms.

As well as being housed and fed, the men were divided into various parts of the army where their civilian skills could be put to good use – although this 'theory' was more honoured in the breach than in practice, and one hears tales of dustmen becoming cooks and hospital porters being sent to signals. Organisation was based upon the combined Arms Division of roughly 17,500 men of all ranks.

At the far end of the scale, each man was allocated to a section of 10 men. 3 sections made up a platoon with 1 officer, 6 NCOs and 30 men. 3 platoons formed 1 company, and 6 companies made up the battalion – being 33 officers and 753 NCOs and men when Battalion HQ officers and the various support groups are added. 3 battalions and additional brigade staff made up the Infantry Brigade and across a typical brigade

there were 2,240 rifles, 175 LMGs, 126 SMGs, 80 piats, 18 3 in mortars, and 48 2 in mortars. The Division had two full infantry brigades and a tank brigade of 44 infantry tanks, 16 Cruiser tanks, 18 close support tanks and 37 scout cars manned by 117 officers and 1,824 men organised into 3 tank battalions of 4 squadrons in each, with each squadron composed of 5 troops of 3 tanks. Attached to them were the artillery: 1 Light Anti-Aircraft regiment with 54 40 mm guns; an Anti-Tank regiment with 48 6-pdrs and 3 field artillery regiments of 36 officers and 194 men, organised into 3

THE WAR AT HOME

The NAAFI wagon. In times of emergency you could always rely upon the NAAFI wagon turning up with a brew and a bite to eat. They met the shattered remains of the BEF off the little boats returning from Dunkirk with char and a wad, and served tea at VE parties all over Europe

The Royal Observer Corps. Often placed in the most exposed of locations, the Royal Observer Corps could sight, plot and relay the position of enemy aircraft. Like the Home Guard, they were volunteers

batteries in each regiment, each of 2 troops with 4 25-pdrs each. In addition, there was a Recce regiment; a Divisional Signals squadron; 4 companies of army service corps; a RAMC unit of 2 field ambulance units with 4 companies in each plus 2 field dressing stations; a body of Royal Engineers with 3 field companies, 1 park company and a postal unit; a RAOC unit of 2 infantry and 1 tank brigade companies; and finally the provost company. This massive formation also had its own Divisional intelligence, field security and HQ defence team. This scheme held good for the first few years of war, but was adapted to cope with changing operational requirements as the war progressed.

The Royal Observer Corps

With such a complicated and intricate structure an efficient communication system was essential. Wireless Telegraphy – WT – or Morse code had been available earlier but it was slow and fraught with error. The introduction of Radio Telegraphy – RT – made the organisation now required both possible and practical. The ability to speak to whomsoever one chose, to issue orders and get information whenever required, all done by speaking to people directly, made command a much easier job, although the lack of secrecy on the air waves was always a problem. However, many men were rapidly trained in using radio communications. Training in general was all the army could do in the early years and this was re-organised by Page and Montgomery and re-equipped largely by the USA despite their 'neutrality'.

During 1937 changes began to be made in the dress of the British fighting man, although the introduction of new uniforms was very slow. Indeed, in 1939/40 many BEF troops looked no different to their fathers in 1914. Finally, however, puttees disappeared along with peaked caps, brass-buttoned coats and even folded and creased trousers. These items were replaced with a much more practical uniform, the battledress. It consisted of a short, khaki, serge blouse, waisted, belted and with concealed buttons. This was worn over the trousers and was nicknamed the 'bum freezer'. It had two breast pockets for personal belongings and ammunition.

The trousers too had external pockets, a large one on the left for maps and a small one below the waist on the right for a first-aid dressing. The legs had buttons at the bottom so that the material could be caught together prior to binding them with strap-on canvas gaiters. These fitted over the ankles and supposedly prevented water running down inside the unchanged, regulation, hard-leather, thirteen-studded army boot. There was also a new greatcoat, fuller, longer and of warmer wool than the old overcoat. A khaki side hat was issued, and dress caps in regimental colours for 'walking out' were available, although these were often not issued but had to be purchased.

Another innovation was the Web Equipment Pattern 37, which went over the uniform. It was based upon a wide waistbelt, onto which were buckled ammunition pouches, shoulder straps to secure two packs, one

215

The introduction of radio telegraphy gave officers the ability to communicate directly with another link in the chain of command, whether one or both were mobile. The open airwaves caused problems with maintaining secure communications

Above, left: 'Bum-freezer' battledress; right:
'Bulling', 'Princes Irene' Regt, Netherlands Brigade

large and one small, which carried rations and spare clothing, a bayonet on the right, a water bottle on the left, a helmet of the 1916 pattern, and an improved design gas mask. It sounds a lot, but was far more comfortable than the old style and the large packs inevitably went on transports.

Transport was a considerable problem, especially shipping men and equipment overseas. During the early '40s most British activity was in North Africa, the Mediterranean and the Far East. Commercial liners were pressed into service as troop ships and guarded by RN escorts; 'Grey Funnel Steamers' took Tommies on world cruises they could never have dreamed about before the war. The Second World War was truly a world war and the men found themselves fighting in all types of terrain, in all parts of the globe. Men from 'the Empire' were also shipped to places and climates far beyond their previous experience and expectations. Indian battalions fought in the rocky deserts of Libya as well as the more familiar jungles of Burma. Canadians, Australians, South Africans and New Zealanders provided large contingents to wherever the fighting proved fiercest, the Anzacs proving a stubborn foe in Tobruk.

Although the butt of 'late again' jibes, the sheer size of the American contribution is daunting: at the end they had 8.3 million men under arms

US PARATROOPERS

American paratrooper wearing the following equipment: MIC helmet, M1942 jumpsuit (official designation Coat, Parachute, Jumper, M1942 and Trouser, Parachute, Jumper, M1942). The gas mask is the Service, Mask, Lightweight M4–10–6. His personal equipment consists of M1936 suspenders and M1936 pistol belt, and he is wearing on his back an M1936 Musett bag. Tied to the front of the suspenders near his left shoulder is a field dressing. The gloves (Horsehair, Riding) were a favourite with US paras. On his right wrist is a wrist compass, and on the pistol belt a pouch for a different compass (Pouch, Compass, Lensatic). Also fixed to the belt is an Mk II fragmentation grenade and just visible on his right thigh is the top of the grenade bag. His weapon is an MI Garand, additional ammunition for which is carried in a bandoleer slung round his chest.

The M3 sub-machine-gun was known as the 'grease gun'

across the world. Recruits began as volunteers until draft machinery was put into place, but they were all treated alike. They went from a home holding depot to a recruit depot for seven or eight weeks of basic training. This was known as a 'boot camp'. Three weeks were given over to intensive drill, both marching and weapons. Then came three weeks of rifle practice with the Garand M1 and the M3 Thompson sub-machine-gun – the 'grease gun'. The last week or two were spent in bayonet practice and close combat. All through camp, the men had to come to terms with the US Army. Its jargon, drills, inspections, duties and routines were drummed into their close-shaven heads. After forty-eight days, and a brief spell of home leave, the recruits were ready to face the war. They were shipped out as batches and kept apart from veterans, especially those from the Pacific theatres, whose 'sloppy appearance', distaste for discipline and distrust of rule books made them 'bad influences'.

The 'gung ho' attitude encouraged by the movie culture and the strong sense of US individualism made for a carefree and almost careless approach to danger. When they transferred to the European theatre, they were full of pride, expectation and a desire to get stuck into the Germans. The Atlantic Ocean and the US media machine sheltered the men from the real war and fostered the image of the movie-star GI going to clean up the gun-toting bad guys in the black Nazi hats. (Text continues on p. 226)

The Americans brought 35 mm Cine and stills cameras as well as their media culture to the battle front

In preparation for the D-Day invasion of Europe, English lanes echoed to the sound of American marching feet

OMAHA – D-Day 'Dog Green' section of Omaha beach. The 1st Battalion of the 116th Infantry suffered horrific casualties. Company 'A' had 91 men killed and as many wounded. Less than 20 men got across the beach to find some form of shelter from the vicious sustained enemy fire

In all, the 116th Regiment lost 800 men on D-Day

In 1944 Britain became a 'tent hotel' for thousands of American and other Allied servicemen as they waited for news of the invasion. Hundreds of acres of farmland disappeared under canvas

Allied commanders used doubles to thwart assassination attempts

The German Army was not full of Nazis. Although this excellently drilled fighting machine was reliant upon Nazi policies to function, many of the soldiers were unaware of the crimes against humanity that were being perpetrated in their name. That is not to state that the men did not share the arrogance of the 'superior race'; indeed their fighting ability was often enhanced by it. They fought with grim determination across the vast plains of central Europe, the deserts of North Africa and the close countryside of western Europe. Like the Allies, they were ordinary men, trained for war and hardened by it, but they had to suffer the dictates of a command structure that made political policy decisions rather than military or humane ones. In Russia, for example, fuel had priority and the German troops endured the winter without sufficient food and with infrequent issues of winter clothing – one battalion reported over 800 cases of frostbite in one day. It is notable that because the German Army was based upon systems, when human failings or weaknesses occurred it often meant complete breakdown, as men were not supposed to fail.

The men at every front suffered tremendously from the pilfering and corruption of the rear echelons, and the official view was that it could not be happening. On most fronts, the men were often left to forage for themselves for all their needs, including food, as the field kitchens could

In Russia fuel had priority and the German Army endured the winter without sufficient food and with infrequent issues of winter clothing

The German Army, too, had its fair share of Military Policemen. Often transferred from the civilian force, they were skilled in detecting and deterring crime among soldiers

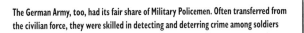

On most fronts, the men were often left to forage for themselves for all their needs, including food

not cope with the demand or the volume of men they had to feed. The uniforms of the various theatres of the war were often very different from the official versions seen in text books or modern films.

This *laissez-faire* attitude of the General Staff towards the men, especially when things were difficult, resulted in horrendous losses. Their numbers were made up by drafts of young men, often in their mid-teens, who had just finished basic training. As the war turned in the Allies' favour, the fighting efficiency of the German Army declined. The veterans of Blitzkrieg were slowly reduced in number – killed, starved, captured or deserted. Political purges had stripped out many potentially capable officers and the whole, once-superb machine was worn and tired. The citizens in arms were ready to become just citizens again.

THEIR WEAPONS

Handguns: Because most development of handguns had taken place in the nineteenth century, work in the early 1900s was focused upon safety features and improving the alloys and steel used in their manufacture. Although handguns were still the weapon of the officers in all arms, they were also issued to tank crews, military police and specialist corps such as the Commandos, whose actions often required close combat and short-range work. They were used in large quantities by all combatant countries during the Second World War, and basically consisted of two types:

Revolvers: These were single-shot weapons with the ammunition contained in a revolving cylinder. Usually holding six rounds, the weapon required re-cocking between each shot and the empty cartridge cases had to be ejected manually before reloading. The reliability of the revolver kept it a firm favourite, with the Webley & Scott 0.45, although first issued in 1915, being preferred along with the Smith & Wesson 0.38.

Automatics: These pistols were in fact semi-automatic, re-cocking after each shot and ejecting the empty cartridge automatically as ammunition was fed up from a six- to ten-round magazine located in the butt. Designs differed little from early models: the Luger P'08 served the Germans well from 1908 onwards along with the Walter PPK; the Americans favoured the Colt & Browning 9 mm; while the British preferred the Enfield No. 2 1932.

The reliability of the revolver had to be offset against its weight, bulk and slower operation, as well as its smaller magazine.

Rifles: These too were single-shot weapons, but the longer barrel and more powerful propellant gave them a much longer range than the effective 20 to 30 yd of the handgun. A steady shot could achieve great accuracy at 500 yd.

The Lee Enfield No. 4 Mk I Calibre .303, ten rounds per magazine

The Royal Norfolk Regiment Bren gun team

The majority of rifles in service with the majority of armies during this period were bolt-action weapons with a ten- to twelve-round magazine. The British Lee Enfield No. 4 Mk I Rifle was issued to the British Army in 1939. It weighed just over 9 lb. It differed little from the Short Model Lee Enfield, but had a special 'battle sight' fitted, for fixed range firing at 200 yd and which could be flipped up into use quickly. The No. 5 Mk I came into production late in the war for service in the Far East where a shorter, lighter weapon proved more useful for close action jungle fighting.

Model	Calibre	Weight (lb/oz)	Magazine Capacity	Effective Range (yd)
Enfield No. 4 Mk I 1939	.303	9 lb 1 oz	10	600
Enfield No. 5 Mk I 1944	.303	7 lb 2 oz	10	400

The Americans entered the war with the Garand Rifle from the Springfield Armoury. It was self-loading, gas-operated and weighed 4.2 kg, or 9½ lb. However, the Americans preferred self-loading carbines and used the pre-war 0.30 calibre, semi-automatic Garand. It was gas-operated and weighed 9½ lb and became the standard arm, used extensively by US troops throughout the war along with the later and lighter Mk 1 Carbine. Originally designed by Winchester, the Mk 1 featured a fifteen-round magazine and weighed 5½ lb. It was remarkably efficient and its modified version, the Mk 2 with a thirty-round magazine and selective fire capability, was a firm favourite at the end of the war among enlisted men and hardened professionals alike, even being carried by some units in Vietnam.

Although reliable and usually well made, the rifle had the drawback of not firing rapidly enough to combat the ever-increasing use of machine-guns. A truly automatic weapon relies upon pressure on the trigger to feed cartridges continually into the breech by recoil or gas operation. The single-shot rifle was excellent for general duties and it had its champions in terms of range, accuracy and in sentiment, but in the close quarter, hectic action that became a typical style of fighting in the 1940s, the automatic was to be the queen of infantry weaponry. The Second World War was the age of the machine-gun.

Automatic weapons: Until the advent of the tank, the medium and heavy machine-gun had been the uncrowned kings of the battlefield, quickly halting any attempt at movement and inducing the stalemate of trench warfare. During the Second World War, machine-guns light, medium and heavy formed part of the equipment of all operational army units for use in both ground and anti-aircraft roles. They were mounted upon tanks and in aeroplanes and the introduction of smaller, lighter versions that could be carried and used by one man meant that speed of movement could be linked to rapid firepower. The British and Soviet Armies favoured the light machine-gun, producing something that was light enough to be carried by men, flexible enough to be bipod-mounted or shoulder-fired, and capable of short rather than sustained bursts of automatic fire at a high cyclic rate. The Russians produced the Degtyarev DT, while the British developed the Bren.

The Bren gun was a gas-operated weapon, first produced by the Czechoslovakian Skoda works but subsequently manufactured at Enfield in Britain. It was introduced to the British Army in 1935 and was distributed at a rate of one per section, so it went to all branches of the army in varying quantities. It fired the standard service .303 cartridge, either singly or automatically at a rate of 450 to 550 rounds per minute according to the adjustment of the gas regulator. It could shoot as far as 2,000 yd but 600 yd was its best range for maximum efficiency. It weighed just over 22 lb including its bipod mount, and it and thirty rounds of ammunition could be carried by two men. Each magazine held twenty-eight rounds and in action it was one man's task to keep swapping the mags. Because of its

The Bren gun, mounted for anti-aircraft use

lightness and strength it became a firm favourite of the forces and the army developed a special vehicle to carry it into action – the unimaginatively named armoured Bren carrier. It could also come equipped with a long-legged tripod mounting for anti-aircraft use, and its naval mounting made it a successful edition to the armament of Coastal Command's MTBs and Air-Sea Rescue launches.

The German and US Armies made no distinction between the light and medium MGs, the Germans using the 7.92 mm MG34 and the Americans the 0.30 calibre Browning in both roles, for ground, tank and anti-aircraft use. The British, however, chose to fill the MMG role with two weapons, the 0.303 in Vickers tripod-mounted gun for ground use and the 7.92 BESA (also of Czech design) for tank weapons.

	Calibre	Weight (lb/oz)	Rate of Fire (rpm)	Method of Operation	Feed	Cooling
LMGs:						
Bren Mk I 1937	.303	22 lb 5 oz	500	Gas	Magazine	Air
Degtyarev DPM 1945	7.62 mm	26 lb 13 oz	530–580	Gas	Air	
Johnson M41	.3	26 lb 13 oz	300–900	Recoil	Magazine	Air
HMGs:						
Degtyarev DShK 1938	12.7 mm	78 lb 8 oz	550	Gas	Belt	Air
Nippon Type 92 1938	7.7 mm	122 lb	450–550	Gas	Strip	Air
Vickers Mk I late '40s	.303	88 lb 8 oz	450–550	Recoil	Belt	Water
GPMGs:						
MG34 1934	7.92 mm	26 lb 11 oz	800–900	Recoil	Belt	Air
MG42 1942	7.92 mm	25 lb 8 oz	1,500	Recoil	Belt	Air
Vehicle mounted MGs:						
Vickers Mk V 1933	.303	58 lb	700	Recoil	Belt	Water
BESA Mk III 1937	7.92 mm	54 lb	75–450	Gas	Belt	Air
Browning M2 US	.50	65 lb 2 oz	800	Recoil	Belt	Air
Browning Mk 2 UK	.303	26 lb 8 oz	500	Recoil	Belt	Air

Paratrooper with Sten gun. This light weapon was produced in large numbers. It was of basic construction and cheap to produce

However, these weapons were too heavy and unwieldy for fast-moving infantry in close combat, as were the rifles and carbines. They needed a weapon that could deliver rapid rates of fire in short bursts, so it was decided by all combatants that an automatic personal weapon of medium range was required, and all sides produced 'miniature' machine-guns for this role. They were known as sub-machine-guns, the first of which to appear was the 0.45 calibre Thompson, a gas-operated weapon fed from a fifty- round drum magazine. (These were the famous 'Tommy guns' of the Chicago mobsters of the 1920s.) It operated on a delayed blowback system, incorporating the H-shaped Blish lock, which was later replaced with a plain belt. It was a deadly close-quarter weapon, with two sculpted hand-grips to help keep it steady while it sprayed bullets at a rate of 700 rounds per minute. Both the British and the American Armies purchased

The Vickers machine-gun

large numbers of Thompsons but, although reliable, it was found to be too heavy and too expensive for general army issue. It was replaced in the British Army by the 9 mm Sten gun; this was a cheap weapon, not overly reliable, being susceptible to frequent mechanism failure, but it was adequate. The men worked out that by putting only 27 of its 9 mm rounds into the 32-round magazine a more steady rate of fire could be achieved and the tendency of the gun to jam was reduced. Despite its drawbacks, the British Army adopted it in 1940 as their close-quarter weapon, with several different versions, and some 2 million were produced by the end of the war, with many being parachuted into Europe for the various resistance groups.

The Germans had a much superior weapon, the 9 mm Schmeisser. Originally designed as a parachutist's weapon, its efficiency and accuracy were so impressive that it became the standard issue. German soldiers could insert all thirty-two of its 9 mm cartridges without much fear of the mechanism jamming, and the weapon itself weighed little more than 4.8 kg, or 10½ lb. It was of excellent design and also fairly cheap to make, and its performance on the Eastern Front prompted the Russians to copy it in vast numbers during the late 1940s and early '50s.

Artillery: During the First World War, the artillery had fought from fixed batteries behind the lines, but the faster, fluid, mobile warfare of the Second World War required faster moving, more mobile artillery, capable of keeping up with the moving front, taking on both armour and infantry,

The Schmeisser MP40 sub-machine-gun

and capable of both direct and indirect fire. Accordingly, light and medium weapons were put onto field mountings capable of being towed at speed across country by specially designed towing vehicles, while others, along with some anti-tank guns, were mounted on armoured self-propelled tracked tank chassis, in large numbers on both sides. The number and types of artillery weapons, both towed and self-propelled, used by Germany and the Allies during the 1940s are far too extensive to be listed fully here. However, this short list shows some of the more numerous British guns:

Model	Weight (tons)	Calibre	Shell Weight (lb)	Muz. Velocity (ft per sec)	Max. Range (yd)
25-pdr Gun Howitzer	1,77	3.45	25	1,700	13,400
3.7 in Mountain Howitzer	0.82	3.7	20	973	6,000
4.5 in BL Medium Gun	5.75	4.5	55	2,250	20,500
5.5 Medium Gun	6.09	5.5	100	1,675	16,200
7.2 BL Heavy Howitzer Mk 4	10.16	7.2	200	1,700	16,900
13.5 BL Superheavy Gun	240	13.5	1,250	2,550	40,000

They arrived at a chosen site and unlimbered, forming a deployed battery or a section of two guns. The gunners rode in the soft-topped lorry with the ammunition – a hazardous duty. However, towards the end of the war the self-propelled gun became a recognised feature. The caterpillar-tracked mobile gun was necessary to match the cross-country speed and flexibility of tank formations and its armour was necessary to give it the equivalent level of protection enjoyed by those who fought alongside it. The recoil problem had been solved during the First World War, but the recoilless field gun was honed to perfection during this period. Some of the more common types of artillery pieces are listed below.

The most popular British field gun was the 25-pdr 3.45 in calibre Mk 2 field gun. This was a gun howitzer, so called because it could fire direct and indirect, with variable propellant charges. It had a circular firing fitted beneath the wheels, which could be dropped in action to permit very rapid traversing, and a good crew could keep up six rounds per minute rapid fire. The 25-pdr used semi-fixed HE, AP shot, smoke and illuminating ammunition, which made it a versatile weapon capable of infantry support or anti-tank duties. It was used in all campaigns of the war in which the British were involved and became famous as Montgomery's 'tank buster', used to crushing effect at the Alamein battle.

The most numerous German gun was the 10.5 cm leFH18 (light field howitzer 18), which remained in service from 1935 to 1945. It too was a versatile weapon and operated on the sliding breech principle with a split trail and twin shovels for dealing with recoil. It had various forms of ammunition, including everything the British 25-pdr could fire, plus incendiary, HEAT and a very strange type, the propaganda shell, which was used to drop political leaflets over a target area.

THEIR ARMOUR

The invention of the internal combustion engine in the late nineteenth century, in combination with that of the caterpillar-type track in the twentieth, enabled the construction of self-propelled weapon carriages with sufficient power reserves to allow the gun crews to be protected by an adequate thickness of armour. The greatly increased use of armoured fighting vehicles on the battlefield revolutionised land warfare from 1917 onwards, and required the industrial production of armour plate in quantity to be rethought and new techniques for the fabrication of armoured structures to be developed.

In Germany, National Socialism exploited the imagery of the gothic knight coupled with industrial might, and most infantrymen wore steel helmets; snipers wore light but strong plates slipped into special pockets in protective jackets; and American aircrew wore a variety of pieces of body armour including bullet-proof waistcoats and a face shield with mail similar to those worn by early tank crews. The tank had played a very large part in

The 25-pdr Mk 2

the Allies' victory in the First World War, but this fact appeared to have been appreciated by only the Germans. Where the defence budgets of the Western allied nations were increasingly squeezed in the 1920s and '30s, that of Germany was steadily increased from 1933 onwards, and it was not until Hitler's take-over of the Rhineland, Austria and Czechoslovakia that Britain and France took notice. The performance of Hitler's tanks in the Spanish Civil War similarly alerted the Soviet government to the dangers poised by these machines so that, by 1939, while France poured resources into the Maginot Line, heavy industry in Britain, Germany and the Soviet Union was concentrating on the design and development of tanks and the production of armour plate.

Armour plate was also required in increasing quantities for the protection of aircrew and aircraft, trucks and trains, as well as warships. However, the main users of armour plate, on a vast scale, were the armoured fighting vehicles, the AFVs. As the anti-armour performance of weapons increased so tank armour had to be thicker to withstand it. To penetrate the thicker armour, an even more powerful gun was required, which necessitated a larger tank with more armour plate, and so the see-saw battle between gun and protection continued. There was also a corollary. All this armour demanded bigger, more powerful engines to keep tanks moving fast

enough to avoid being easy to hit. Designs too sought to make the tank less of a target by adopting the medieval principle of directing hits away as glancing blows off sloping surfaces.

The Soviet T-34 pioneered the use of sloping armour. It was a very successful tank, combining speed with a powerful gun, excellent handling mobility and good cold weather performance, and the Russians produced them in hitherto undreamed of numbers. They first appeared on the Eastern Front in 1941 and so impressed the German High Command that they called for copies, and in large quantities, to issue to the panzer units. However, the scientific and political answer was the Tiger, a much heavier tank with thicker armour and even more powerful armament, but which was very slow to build and very expensive. They were never manufactured in anything like the numbers required to stop the T-34. It was the quantity of armour that finally defeated the panzers. The Soviet T-34 and the US M4 Sherman were produced in numbers of which the German armament industry could only dream, and although the Tigers and Panthers were individually more effective, they were too complicated and German industry was under too heavy an attack for adequate numbers to be manufactured and for all the 'bugs' to be eliminated from them.

To list every type of tank used in the Second World War would be a study in its own right, but the following table features some of the more important:

Model	Weight (tons)	Crew	Speed (mph)	Ops Range (miles)	Armament	Armour (mm)
Vickers Mk 6 1936	5.2	3	35	130	1 × 5 in MG 1 × MG	14
Cruiser A9 Mk 1 1938	12.8	6	25	150	1 × 2-pdr 1 × MG	14
Crusader 2 1939	19	5	27	100	1 × 2-pdr 2 × MGs	49
Valentine 3 1940	16	4	15	90	1 × 2-pdr 1 × MG	65
Churchill 3 1941	39	5	15	90	1 × 6-pdr 2 × MGs	102
Grant 1941	27.7	6	24	120	1 × 75 mm 1 × 37 mm	51
Stuart 6 1942	14.7	4	36	100	1 × 37 mm 3 × MGs	64
Cromwell 1942	27.5	5	40	17	1 × 6-pdr 2 × MGs	102
Sherman 5C 1944 Firefly	32.1	4	25	100	1 × 17-pdr 2 × MGs	51
Centurion 1 1945	49	4	21	65	1 × 17-pdr 1 × 20 mm	152

Armoured cars:

Model	Weight (tons)	Crew	Speed (mph)	Ops Range (miles)	Armament	Armour (mm)
Daimler 1941	7.5	3	50	205	1 × 2-pdr 1 × MG	16
Humber 1941	6.7	3	40	250	1 × 15 mm MG 1 × MG	15
AEC 1942	11	3	35	250	1 × 2-pdr 2 × MGs	57

THEIR FIGHTING

The Second World War established the potential of the tank with its fire-power and rapid manoeuvrability. Supported by aircraft, it could smash through a defensive line such as trenches, no matter how complex they might be, and strike deep into enemy territory and inflict crushing military defeats, rolling forward continually and denying an enemy time to regroup, reorganise or, indeed, rearm. The war also showed the value of shock troops using stormtrooper tactics, which advocated that men went swiftly into action and delivered a powerful blow at a specific point, eliminating an objective and awaiting reinforcements to take over the mopping up and exploitation of the won situation. These actions by ground or airborne forces, armed with light machine-guns or sub-machine-guns, demonstrated the supremacy of surprise, speed and firepower over static defence, even in depth, which could be outflanked or smashed by the new offensive techniques.

The infantry were trained in the latest tactics used during the First World War, by which small groups of men with sub-machine-guns rushed short distances under the covering fire of each other. It was a tactic very similar to that worked out by Sir John Moore when training the light regiments at Shorncliff, which the British called 'gaining ground in pairs by the alternation of fire and advance', and the Americans 'the buddy system'. It was most effective when used in skirmishes by single-shot armed professionals, and equally useful to the less experienced using LMGs or Tommy guns and hand-grenades.

The general purpose machine-gun, or GPMG, was evolved to provide infantry static support, but the fixed machine-gun too had lost its supremacy. It had been eclipsed by the use of the light mortar, the strike aircraft that could both strafe and bomb, and AFVs that carried HMGs but moved rapidly, providing support in critical situations and being able to respond efficiently to any new threat that arose. Tanks were, of course, the epitome of weaponry for this fast-moving, hard-hitting warfare, their variety of guns and thickness of armour providing each type with a specific tactical role ranging from spearheading attacks, to flying around in defensive swarms. Armoured personnel carriers made use of the lessons of the tank and could deliver the infantryman in relative safety at a chosen strategic point ready to fight. The infantryman now had the means to fight on the move and avoid becoming bogged down.

On a grander scale, this war of rapid and powerful movement was called Blitzkrieg, or lightning war. The Germans concentrated the tanks of their panzer divisions into an offensive phalanx and, using dive-bombers as flying artillery, aimed the thrust at a perceived weak point in an enemy's defences, smashed it and swept through to cause havoc and confusion behind the lines. Meanwhile, the mechanised infantry poured into the gap to exploit and consolidate the gain. Given the spares and the fuel, Blitzkrieg could fight its way forward for 30 to 50 miles in twenty-four hours.

The speed, power and range of the motor vehicle and the aeroplane were all vastly superior to anything horse-drawn but it was the speed of communications that made it all hang together and operate effectively. A general in action could call for an air strike at a critical moment to eliminate a pocket of resistance and, within half an hour, the dive-bombers would obliterate it and the advance could roll forward again. Radio intelligence and speed of decision-making kept apace with the speed at which situations changed. This was a revolution in battlefield tactical ability. Erhard Milch said of Blitzkrieg, 'The real secret is speed, speed of attack through speed of communication'. Blitzkrieg was the result of technology delivering 'real time war'.

The most famous exponent of these armoured tactics, Erwin Rommel, nevertheless realised the limitations of armour in defence, where he relied upon anti-tank mines, covered by anti-tank guns, to channel attacking armour into the chosen killing ground. He was quick also to appreciate the importance of the logistic support for advancing armour being able to keep up with the attack; it was a lesson learned the hard way by early British commanders in the Western Desert campaign who had armoured formations that ran too far ahead of their replenishment echelons and became easy meat for enemy tanks. The Allies also suffered from having an inflexible command structure, poor radio equipment and slow procedure, as well as an inadequate recovery system. Nowhere were the results of these lessons put to greater effect than at the second battle of El Alamein by Montgomery, who refused to attack until more than sufficient stocks of ammunition, petrol, water and food had been amassed to support the British breakthrough and subsequent pursuit through Libya to Tunis in 'Operation Supercharge'. Montgomery's own blitzkrieg concentrated armour push went through the German centre, supported by air cover and employing flank pressure via the infantry. Real time warfare with excellent communications by wireless dramatically changed the soldiers' experience of war. They were now part of a coordinated machine that worked when and where the commander ordered. This British victory by a highly trained force changed the soldiers' and units' morale dramatically and gave them the confidence to fight successful campaigns in Sicily, Italy and North-West Europe.

During the opening phases of the war, the infamous Ju87 Stuka dive-bomber wreaked havoc with soldiers on the ground in the battle area, while the Dornier, Junkers and Heinkel medium and heavy bombers ranged further afield to drop their deadly cargoes over targets on the British mainland. But German air supremacy suffered its first defeat in the summer of 1940 at the hands of the RAF's Spitfire and Hurricane pilots, supported by the miracle of radar and access to the top secret Enigma decrypts.

Until the advent of the North American P-51 Mustang in 1942, the Allies had lacked the capability of a long-range high performance fighter to take the war back into the very heart of Germany. It took the Americans to design the Mustang, but the British to realise its fullest potential when fitted with the Rolls-Royce Merlin engine. Equipped with long-range jettisonable fuel tanks, the USAAF's P-51s could fly all the way to Berlin as daylight fighter escorts to its B-17 and B-24 bombers. Once over 'The Big City' they would jettison their drop-tanks to dogfight with the Luftwaffe fighters, and then return home to bases in England.

The P-51 could tangle with anything the Germans could put into the air and in most cases it would win. It represented a quantum leap forward in air warfare and was one factor that enable the Allies to maintain their air supremacy over the Luftwaffe.

The P-51 was also a symbol of the mechanisation of war and the way in which it could not be contained to a small battlefield. Weapons production copied the US car industry in fast, economic practices. Small arms, artillery, aeroplanes, tanks, ships, submarines and rockets all streamed from the factories of the Allied nations, while the money spent on scientific research enabled another great 'leap forward' in man's ability to kill other men – the discovery of nuclear fission and the production of the Atomic bomb. In August 1945 it brought Japan to its kenes, as economic and scientific might conveyed a supreme example of total war to a popular still practising the Bushido cult of the warrior élite. High in the skies over Hiroshima the men of the *Enola Gay* faced no real personal danger as they opened their bomb-doors and released the single bomb that was to mark the eclipse of 'The Fighting Man' and trumpet the triumph of the philosophy of total involvement and the technology of total destruction.

'The return of the patrol'. A French barn gives temporary respite during the advance after D-Day

Chance for a wash and shave, in a small mess tin . . .

. . . and to tend the wounded . . .

... before the advance over hostile ground

Advancing in 'open order' to minimize casualties if fired upon

CORPORAL SIDNEY (BASHER) BATES VC – PERRIER RIDGE, FRANCE, 6 AUGUST 1944

B' Company of the 1st Battalion, Royal Norfolk Regiment, had suffered an accurate artillery and mortar bombardment and now faced 50 to 60 German soldiers of 10th Panzer Division. Corporal Bates commanded the right forward section of the left

Forward Company; his section had already suffered casualties. The German attack started in earnest and the situation was getting desperate. Corporal Bates' Bren gun 'buddy' was shot through the head beside him.

Seizing the Bren gun, Corporal Bates stood up and charged at the enemy and was hit almost immediately; he dropped to the ground but got up and ran on . He was hit a second time, fell, and scrambled to his feet once again

Still moving forward and firing from the hip, he dismayed the enemy machine-gunners and riflemen who began to fall back, but the mortars kept falling

He received a severe wound from a mortar splinter that was eventually to prove fatal and he fell for the last time. He still kept firing until his strength left him. He was twenty-three years old.

The Norfolks won the day

Firing the 2 in mortar. The Royal Norfolk Regiment

The British Lee Enfield No. 4 Mk I Calibre .303, 10 rounds per magazine

The Piat – Portable Infantry Anti Tank

THE SECOND WORLD WAR

The American air drop. The 82nd Airborne Division quickly found their position on the ground. The German reaction was slow. However, some drops were inaccurate, men landing on marshy ground or even in the sea

VE-Day, Dover, 1945. 'You must remember this...'

VE-Day, somewhere in Europe. At the end of a gruelling trek through grim days, a few words home . . .

. . . and a photo of the lads . . .

... to re-live the deprivations, bravery and camaraderie of the Fighting Man ...

... a permanent record for generations to come ...

... lest we forget

USEFUL ADDRESSES

Living History Photography
All the photographic images in this book were produced by Paul Lewis Isemonger. These and thousands of others from an extensive photo-library are available at reasonable cost for commercial and non-commercial use. Special low prices for schools and re-enactment groups. All pictures come fully captioned and include the name of the re-enactment group.

Living History Photography/Photo-Library
Park Wood House
163 Thrupp Lane
Far Thrupp
Stroud
Glos. GL5 2EQ
Tel: 01453 886140

'Sharpes Peninsula' Battlefield Tours
Follow in the footsteps of Wellington's Army along with Rifleman Moore to the sites of victory in Portugal and Spain.

Midas Tours
Tel: 01883 744955

Paul Meekins Military and History Books
Second-hand and new; Roman to Second World War. Large selection of Napoleonic and American Civil War. *An excellent and professional service.* For catalogue send two first-class stamps to:

34 Townsend Road
Tiddington
Stratford-upon-Avon
Warks. CV37 7DE
Tel: 01789 295086

Chris Collingwood
Chris Collingwood has worked professionally in animation, advertising and publishing for over twenty years. He now concentrates on the historical and military world. Working mainly in oils, he has a strong feel for historical detail, both in painting technique and in-depth subject research. He can be contacted for private and commercial commissions through the Historic Art Company.

Historic Art Company
The Historic Art Company was formed in 1992 to publish and promote the work of Chris Collingwood. The company helps to resolve both private and commercial commissions and works closely with historical societies, publishers, museums and the re-enactment market.

Historic Art Company
Ashleigh House
236 Wokingham Road
Reading
Berks. RG6 1JS
Tel: 0118 926 1236/867252
Fax: 0118 9314432

Sarah Juniper, Cordwainer
Exquisite and authentic hand-made boots and shoes, using traditional techniques.

Tel: 01453 545675

HMS *Trincomalee* Trust
For the preservation of the 1817 frigate HMS *Trincomalee* (featured in this book).

Jackson Dock
Hartlepool
Cleveland TS24 0SQ

Jackson Dock
Hartlepool Historic Quay
Hartlepool
Cleveland TS24 0SQ

Antique Newspapers
Specialists in newspapers from 1665 to 1865. *Very helpful.*

PO Box 396
Guernsey
Channel Islands GY1 3FW
Tel: 01481 712990
Fax: 01481 725168

Marcus Music
Manufacturers and suppliers of rope-tensioned drums, bodrans and tabors, as well as other historical musical instruments. SAE for catalogue to:

Marcus Music
Tredegar House
Newport
Gwent NP1 9YW
Tel: 01633 815612
Fax: 01633 816979

The Living History Register
Newsletters
Interesting articles on historical subjects plus re-enactment events diary. A recent copy gave detailed instructions on how to construct a fifteenth-century bench and details of Victorian underpinnings, plus a short history of the English court jester.

Subscriptions
Pat Poppy and Roger Emmerson
56 Wareham Road
Lytchet Matravers
Poole
Dorset BH16 6DS

Quartermasterie
Specialists in replica historical artefacts. A wide range of items in linen, horn, iron, tin, wool, pottery, leather, pewter, glass, brass, etc. *High quality items intended for re-enactment but worth collecting in their own right.*
Ian Skipper
Flat 1 Shelley Court
4 Lovelace Road
Surbiton
Surrey KT6 6NP

Albion Small Arms
Maker of fine reproduction muskets and guns. *High quality craftsman-ship.*

Ron Curley
21 Green Lane
Shelfield
Walsall WS4 1RN
Tel: 01922 684964

Past Tents

Reproduction tentage to suit any period. Specialising in late medieval English, American Civil War and Napoleonic designs. A5 SAE for catalogue to:

Past Tents
Hill View Bungalow
Main Street
Clarborough
Retford
Notts. DN22 9NJ
Tel/Fax: 01777 869821

Call to Arms

A listings and contact magazine for most things connected with re-enactment.

Call to Arms
7 Chapmans Crescent
Chesham
Bucks. HP5 2QU
Tel: 01494 7484271

English Heritage Specials Events

The very best in re-enactment from Romans and Celts to Second World War, small living history events to huge displays of martial skills, equipment and day-to-day life in camps, as well as historical entertainment and dance/ music events. All events are based in or around English Heritage properties. *Highly recommended if you want to see life as it really was. Take your camera.*

Special Events information line: 0171 973 3396
General enquiries on English Heritage: 0171 973 3434

St Dunstan's

Caring for men and women blinded in the service of their country.

Contact: Neil M.J. Swan
St Dunstan's – Room A7
FREEPOST WD2
12–14 Harcourt Street
London W1A 4XB

Double Time

Specialists in historical interpretations.

Alison Roddham BSc
1 Golden Noble Hill
Colchester
Essex CO1 2AG
Tel: 01206 768517

Past Pleasures

In association with Wallis Productions. Historical interpretations and consultancy.

Mark Wallis MA, Director
Abbots Cottage
Old Portsmouth Road
St Catherine's
Guildford
Surrey GU2 5EB
Tel/Fax: 01483 450914

Stichting Historische Militaria

Secretariaat:
Akker 18–1841 GS Stompetoren
Tel: (072) 503 92 01

Costume and Dressmaker

The magazine for the serious dressmaker.

Mary Denise Smith
4500 19th St #298
Boulder CO 80304, USA
Tel: (303) 546 6223

High Definition Printing

High quality black and white processing.

Avening Mill
Avening
Glos. GL8 8LU
Tel: 01453 832889

Hautbois

Historical interpretation musicians. Any period from fourteenth to nineteenth century inclusive.

J.K. and H.J. Heavisides
The Post Office
Horsefair
Boroughbridge
N. Yorks. YO5 9AA

Ancient Armouries

Armour, weapons and chainmail.

Dean Goulden
Archery and Crossbow Specialist

33 Scholars Avenue
Hinchingbrooke
Huntingdon PE18 6GP
Tel: 01480 383713

Hector Cole

Ironwork, medieval blade and arrowsmith.

The Mead
Great Somerford
Chippenham
Wilts. SN15 5JB
Tel: 01666 825794

Historical Management Associates Ltd

Feasts, displays, consultancy, publishing.

Stuart Peachey
117 Farleigh Road
Backwell
Bristol BS19 3PG
Tel: 012775 463041

The Leather Man

Medieval drinking vessels, fifteenth-century style jewellery, caskets, shields.

H. Phil Quallington
5 The Blanes
Ware
Herts. SG12 0XA
Tel: 01920 461304

Petty Chapman

Natural fibre textiles, historical patterns and costume accessories.

Dave Rushworth and Lindy Pickard
20 Macaulay Road
Huddersfield
W. Yorks. HD2 2US
Tel: 01484 512968

Mark Taylor and David Hill

Glassmakers specialising in Roman period style ware.

Unit 11 Project Workshops
Lains Farm
Quarley
Andover
Hants. SP11 8PX
Tel: 01264 889688

Trinity Court Potteries
Makers of replica pottery and tiles

Jim and Emma Newboult
Headon Place
65 Cobwell Road
Retford
Notts. DN22 7DD
Tel: 01777 708782

Robin Wood
Pole-lathe bowl turner, designs based on archaeological finds.

Lee Farm Cottage
Upper Booth
Edale
Derbyshire S33 7ZJ
Tel: 01433 670321

Artifex Pewter
Reproduction pocket sundials, cutlery, coins, jewellery, etc. *The very highest standard of work.*
Hopton Cangeford
Ludlow
Shropshire
Tel: 0158 482 3304

Simon Dunn
Reproduction cabinet maker.

Wynnstay Cottage
Lamin Gap Lane
The Fosse
Cotgrave
Notts. NG12 3HG
Tel: 0949 81743

Manchester Metropolitan University
Practical four-day courses with accompanying lectures on costume history.

Gill Tromans
The Manchester Metropolitan University
Hollings Faculty
Old Hall Lane
Fallowfield
Manchester M14 6HR
Tel: 0161 2472662

Richard York
Musician, teacher, enabler, performer, historical and traditional music and social history, with enthusiasm and a variety of instruments.

1 Exmoor Close
Abington Vale
Northampton NN3 3AU
Tel: 0604 39581

Re-enactment Groups Featured in this Book

Napoleonic Wars

The Historical Maritime Society
The only group re-enacting the Royal Navy and Royal Marines around the year 1805. *Enlist today – avoid impressment!*

Chris Jones
3 Bell Hill
Lindal in Furness
Ulverston
Cumbria LA12 0NF
Tel: 01229 463892
e.mail: 75337.1362@compuserve.com

9th (East Norfolk) Regiment of Foot
K. Phillips
Plumtree Cottage
Winslow Road
Granborough
Bucks. MK18 3NJ

12th (Prince of Wales) Light Dragoons
M. Render
Jasmine Cottage
Fern Hill
nr Glemsford
Suffolk CU10 7PR

15th or Kings Light Dragoons (Hussars)
Geoff Potts
Calcot House
Calcot Lane
Curdridge
nr Botley
Southampton SO3 2BN

42nd Royal Highland Regiment
Pipe Sergeant Walker
Tel: 0181 505 3842

95th (Rifles) Regiment of Foot
L. Handscombe
48 Mutton Place
Prince of Wales Road
London NW1 8DF

Military Music Re-enactors Society
17 Booth Street
Handsworth
Birmingham B21 0NG

21ème de Ligne
Chris Durkin
22 Swallow Street
Oldham
Lancs. OL8 4LD

1er Regiment de Chasseurs à Cheval de Ligne, 1er Escadron
Mike Grove
Upper Woodhouse Farm
Holmbridge
W. Yorks. HD7 1QR

45ème de Ligne
David Prior
29 Bayley Court
Winnersh
Wokingham
Berks. RG11 5HT

Napoleonic Association
Michael Freeman, Chairman
5 Thingwall Drive
Irby
Wirral
Merseyside L61 3XN

American Civil War

Southern Skirmish Association
PO Box 485
Swindon SN2 6BF

28th Massachusetts Regiment Vol. Infantry
Jerry Cooke
99 Taunton Road
Bridgewater
Somerset TA6 6AD
Tel: 01278 429038

7th Virginia Cavalry CSA
John Maddocks
40 Jerkins Avenue
St Albans
Herts. AL2 3RY

4th Michigan Cavalry
54 Fort Picklecombe
Torpoint
Cornwall PL10 1JB
Tel: 01752 823057

Victorian/Colonial Wars

Diehard Company, Victorian Military Society
Tim Rose
21 Addison Way
North Bersted
Bognor Regis
W. Sussex PO22 9HY

First World War

Great War Society
Mr G. Carefoot, Chairman
18 Risedale Drive
Longridge
Lancs. PR3 3SB

Second World War

The Royal Norfolk Regiment
Neil Storey, Chairman
17 Stacy Road
Norwich
Norfolk NR3 1JN

US 82nd Airborne Reconstruction Group
One of many groups who can be contacted through:

Second World War Living History Association
M.J. West, Secretary
48 Roe Green Lane
Hatfield
Herts. AL10 0RZ
Tel: 01707 264760

INDEX